Grace's Mirror

Healing for Perfectionists

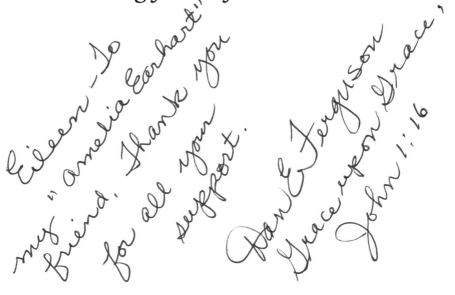

Eileen – To my "Amelia Earhart" friend. Thank you for all your support.

Dan E Ferguson
Grace upon Grace,
John 1:16

DAN FERGUSON

PAGE PUBLISHING, INC.
New York, NY

First originally published by Page Publishing, Inc. 2017

ISBN 978-1-64082-810-0 (Paperback)
ISBN 978-1-64082-811-7 (Digital)

Printed in the United States of America

CONTENTS

ACKNOWLEDGMENTS

I am immensely grateful to the late Dr. Don Joy, my seminary professor and friend. He read the entire original manuscript and was quite encouraging about publishing it. I still keep ten of his published books on my shelf. We grew close while meeting once a week with six other seminary students during all three years of seminary. Richard Foster was a great teacher in a Writing for Publication class at Friends University after seminary. He also inspired me with *Celebration of Discipline* and his other books. I am grateful to HarperCollins Publishers for permission to print eight differences between true service and self-righteous service from Foster's *Celebration of Discipline*. Penney Schwab served as executive director of United Methodist Mexican American Ministries; she took time from an extremely busy schedule to read the original manuscript three times and offer helpful editorial changes.

I am indebted to fellow grad students at Graduate Theological Foundation. Catherine Gilbert heartily endorsed the book from the beginning. Loretta Anderson and Rabbi Allan Tuffs also provided inspiration for this book. The staff at the Cimarron Public Library worked hard to find me books used for reference. A huge thank you goes to Doris Phelps, Margaret Ramsey, Sandy Unruh, and Jeanette Steinkuhler. I am grateful to some wonderful, loving people in United Methodist Churches where I served as pastor, including Wichita Wesley, Great Bend First, Douglass, Rock, Cimarron, Kalvesta, Coffeyville First/St. James, Wichita West Heights, Pratt, and Marion Eastmoor.

Thank you so much to the tremendous staff at Page Publishing: Lindsay Hasbrouck, Stacy Tatters, the Page designer, copy editor, cover artist, and publicity team.

To my best support: thank you to my family. Daughters Rachel and Andrea helped with the technical preparation of the manuscript. Andrea shared her knowledge from her job in interpreting the contract. My wife, Glenda, sacrificed for and supported the book; thank you for your impressive ideas and content. And most of all, thank you to God for inspiring, motivating, and reminding me to persevere!

CHAPTER ONE

Hooked by Perfection

"There is no perfection. It's really the world's greatest con game; it promises riches and delivers misery."

—David Burns

The frown on Andrea's face surprised her mother and me. As Andrea quietly opened the back door after school, she looked brokenhearted. She enjoyed life as the happy-go-lucky type: spontaneous, easygoing, witty. On most days, she skipped between two fences and home from school—only a half block away. Usually she met us with a smile, despite a gap where two front teeth were missing. This six-year-old could make us laugh when things got tense. That sullen look of dismay did not paint an accurate picture of our daughter's usual countenance.

We felt fortunate to live in the small community of Cimarron, Kansas—population about three thousand—where we didn't have to worry about her safety as she walked home from school. Almost everyone watched out for the other folks in our town. We even let our daughters walk downtown to Clark's Drugstore for a black-and-white ice-cream sundae. It was a close-knit community.

Her mother, Glenda, was known for dressing both daughters to a perfect tee. On this day two weeks into first grade, Andrea wore a light-pink blouse with a light-blue denim skirt. Her hair in pigtails was framed by light-pink ribbons matching her blouse. She was also dressed in light-pink socks above blue denim shoes. With a sprinkling of freckles across her nose, Andrea resembled a larger-than-life doll, even though the toothless gap reminded us she was growing up. Two years earlier, Mrs. Seal, her preschool teacher, had advised us that she had seen a change in Andrea. She had seemed shy at first, but once she got into the model kitchen, Mrs. Seal said, "She came out of her shell." We had seen her personality become more outgoing at home too.

One evening, Glenda asked Andrea to go to the garage and bring her the broom. It was hanging by two nails high above the first grader's reach. She began to jump in an effort to touch the bottom of the broom hard enough to dislodge it. Time after time, her efforts failed. But she kept trying. In desperation, she stopped, took a deep breath, and leaped again. Boom! We heard the broom crashing down on the cement floor of the garage. Out came a line Andrea had heard in the past. "By jove, I think I've got it"—in a slight British brogue.

When it came to a love for animals, Andrea was born with a compassion for every creature in sight. When her Aunt Avis gave us a Sheltie that an elderly woman couldn't care for any longer, Andrea was the first of us to look after Lady.

Another opportunity came Andrea's way when Aunt Avis told her to pick out a puppy that Avis would buy. Andrea said, "I want a puppy I can hold in my hand."

They shopped until Andrea faced a difficult decision. She couldn't decide if she wanted the Chihuahua or the Shih Tzu. She already loved them both. It was not greed causing Andrea to ask, "Aunt Avis, can I have both of them?" But we thanked Avis that she could afford one puppy.

Two months later, Andrea added a tiny box turtle to the list of pets under her care. Her sister, Rachel—five years older—had a friend, Kirk, who lived down the hill from us, next to a lake. Kirk[1] seined the little turtle out of the lake and then gave it to Andrea. She fed it lettuce, gave it water, and watched over it as it lived in a small cardboard box. We began suggesting to Andrea that the turtle would be more comfortable and live longer in its natural habitat. Finally, she made a better decision on her own. As she addressed the turtle, she cried, "I don't want to, but I'm going to have to let you go."

Many times, we laughed at Andrea's quips. We needed her humor to lighten up the rest of the family. Later we discovered why. The Briggs-Myers personality type indicator has a scale that measures judgment versus perception. A better description of the judgment side of the scale points to one who lives a planned, orderly, disciplined way of life. The perception score could be defined as one who is flexible, spontaneous, impulsive. The other three of us in the family scored extremely high on the judgment scale, while Andrea ended up in the perception category. We perceived Andrea as a gift to her family of strict disciplinarians.

On this particular day, when Glenda and I saw Andrea walking through the back door in slow baby steps with her head down, we had to wonder why. We just weren't accustomed to seeing the scowl on her face. Had one of her classmates cut her down with a rude comment? Had her teacher, Mrs. Coles, said something to offend her? We couldn't imagine that she had copied a classmate's paper because she was the independent type. More likely, we wondered if she had let another student see her paper.

Andrea said nothing, unloading an inch-thick stack of papers from her backpack onto the kitchen counter. Glenda and I quickly leafed through them. They were all perfect except two papers with one correction on each. Tears streaming down her face, Andrea whispered, "I don't deserve to watch TV today."

She had expected to ace the first grade. Maybe even the next eleven grades. No mistakes. Only a perfect score all the way through school would suffice.

Andrea was not the only one expecting a perfect score. We as family knew lots of other persons who set standards that were beyond human achievement, standards of the typical perfectionist. We even knew of three more in our immediate family! Perfectionists were unanimous in our household. Perfectionists are all around us. I know people who expect to win every game, who expect an A in every course, who expect more than the real world can deliver. How ironic that in a suffering world—a world of cruel reality—so many expect everything to be perfect! I talk to someone almost every day who confesses a battle with perfectionism. Others show the same symptoms but tend to deny perfectionistic tendencies.

Perfectionism is a major plague in our culture. David Burns found that half the population would be classified as "clearly a perfectionist."[2] A survey conducted by David Stoop revealed that 84 percent admitted they were perfectionistic in some way.[3] Counselors agree that nearly every patient has problems related to perfectionism. In his counseling practice, Stoop discovered "that woven into the fabric of almost every problem that people brought to me was a pattern of perfectionism."[4] No one need look very far to see that perfectionism torments a major portion of our society.

Perfectionism strikes persons from all segments of society. James Jolliff maintains that it is, for the most part, not tied to "intelligence, social class, or ethnic groups. It is just as common to one sex as the other."[5] It preys upon nearly everyone at one time or another. Jolliff further says, "Most human beings manifest some perfectionism in some ways at some time."[6] Perfectionism cuts a wide swath on planet earth.

Perfectionism is much more prominent today than it was in the days the apostle Paul sailed the Mediterranean Sea on his missionary journeys. Yet the Bible presents evidence that Paul too struggled with perfectionism. Consider that he makes a list of his accomplishments in Philippians 3:3–6 (New International Version). These include among others: "in regard to the law, a Pharisee; as for zeal, persecuting the church; as for righteousness based on the law, faultless." Much like the perfectionist, the all-encompassing quest for the Pharisee was to accomplish a "faultless" record in keeping every letter of the law. Paul was sure he has been perfect in his pursuit of righteousness. Paul was a perfectionist in keeping the law.

On the other hand, Paul later admits his imperfection in that same chapter: "Not that I am already perfect" (3:12). His words in that same epistle suggest his happiness in every circumstance, something unusual for perfectionists. He writes, "For I have learned to be content with whatever I have" (4:11b). These verses point to Paul's battle with perfectionism as a Pharisee, but also to his eventual healing over it.

Paul's recovery from perfectionism began when he was suddenly converted on the road to Damascus (Acts 9:1–9). Ananias couldn't believe this was the same man who had been intent on killing Christians (Acts 9:13–15). Others couldn't believe it either (9:21). But Paul received God's grace and was changed into a recovering perfectionist. He started the healing process over perfectionism when he was transformed into a follower of Jesus Christ and put his life as a Pharisee behind him.

It can take two years of therapy for a perfectionist to know healing. A licensed therapist knows the value of starting the perfectionist on a treatment called cognitive behavioral therapy (also known as CBT). During CBT, the therapist concentrates upon your inner thoughts (those things you can control). The goal is to keep from focusing on your outer circumstances (those things over which you have little control). The patient works at recognizing new triggers to unwanted actions and seeking options toward desired, improved behaviors. That therapy itself can be immensely intensive.

It's not realistic to expect this book to give the same healing as two years of therapy, but I'll offer some practical ways to conquer perfectionism in these chapters. We'll look at some down-to-earth tips that will steer a perfectionist toward healing. We'll discover how perfectionism develops and then find realistic ways to overcome it.

We'll explore what the Bible and the devotional classics say about perfection. We will search for a mirror that is capable of making the perfectionist happy. No quick fix, this process will take time before healing occurs.

How could we help Andrea? We as her parents hoped that we hadn't expected too much from her. We prayed that we hadn't set the bar too high. We vowed to work at assuring her that we accepted her, mistakes or not. And we could learn to avoid an example of heavy-handed parenting right next door.

CHAPTER TWO

The Parental Push

> "A common story among "'crazy'" folk is their incessant efforts over many years to rear perfect children."
>
> —James Jolliff

Our neighbor—we'll call him Mark—was always ready to play mental hockey with theological issues, always looking for a healthy debate over abortion, the Second Coming, or some such issue. He was skilled at verbal sparring, successfully finding an angle to provoke me to a debate. But he was no churchgoer. His first priority was sports. He never missed playing in a softball or basketball game. Competition was his first love, and that's what he was pushing for when he brought up controversial issues.

Mark made sure he was the coach for his daughters' sports teams. In coach pitch he backed up close to second base and threw like he was Nolan Ryan to his daughters. For everyone else, he pitched from the pitcher's rubber. Each day he demanded that all three daughters sweat through fifty sit-ups and fifty push-ups, along with several other exercises. He had similar expectations for how many times the basketball had to swish through the hoop daily.

On the evening before the elementary track meet, the entire family runs around the track. Dad conducts time trials! He gazes intently at a stopwatch and calls out split times. Mom barks orders to make sure the pace is fast enough. This training exercise lasts until 10:00 at night.

The next day, the track meet didn't bring the results those dedicated parents expected. I can't forget—though I've tried—a vivid picture of the parents at the finish line. Video camera in hand, mother watched her daughter finish second. Since it wasn't their daughter who broke the tape, both mother and father walked away as if the daughter didn't even exist.

It's only natural for parents to want their children to excel. But too many parents play the super coach role. These parents give the impression that their self-esteem depends upon how well the child performs. For the child, life soon becomes a performance to please Dad, Mom, or both. A pushy parent can easily expect more than the child has the ability to accomplish.

Consider both extremes of the success syndrome, extremes we know well through our older daughter, Rachel. In fourth grade, her dreams turned into reality. At the elementary track meet, Rachel broke school records in the seventy-five-yard dash and the long jump and anchored the winning relay team. Undoubtedly, this was due to the superb coaching I gave her! In reality, I did nothing to prepare her except measure her step for the long jump, make sure she was in bed by nine, and encourage her to eat healthy meals.

We were proud of her success. We were prouder, though, that she was gracious to those who finished behind her—and we affirmed that. We strive to work at encouraging our children. Building self-esteem is a high priority.

Yet we try to stop short of over-affirming the achievement itself. That gives the child the idea that winning is more important than showing a gracious attitude in losing or genuine humility in winning.

We want our children to know that our love is unconditional. Why? Because perfectionism develops when the child senses the parent is more concerned with the final result of any contest than with the parent-child relationship. We do everything possible to ensure our daughters feel that our relationships with them are more important than any achievement.

Two years later, the results were just the opposite at Rachel's sixth grade track meet. She finished last in every race and second in the long jump. How do parents handle it when the child expects first and ends up last?

Our approach was to offer the same affirmation we would give for a first-place finish. We want our children to know our love does not change, and it doesn't depend upon any time, score, grade, or result. We also remind Rachel of recent successes in other activities. I tell Rachel that we don't need to make excuses, but that I honestly believe that she is in a growth spurt that affects speed. The long-term effects from this track meet were far from defeat. We learn much more from losses than victories. Whatever the results—first or last—the most significant agenda is to support the child!

Some people are born with more competitive drive than others.

But more often, that killer instinct is taught by parents who place impossible expectations upon their children. Once competition has been ingrained, we no longer need someone else to battle. We can compete with ourselves. Ellen Stern states, "Having been raised on competition, we've each got a running scoreboard that acts as a constant reminder that we're never ahead."[1]

Is it any surprise that the most common cultural cause for perfectionism in our society is competition? Competition may have pushed us toward essential learning in school, but usually we have expended too much energy trying to keep up with someone else. The healthier route is to accept ourselves for who we are rather than repeatedly feeling as though others are better.

It's always futile to spend time worrying about how well others perform. When we endlessly compare ourselves to others, we can't develop ourselves. Perfectionism is fueled by perpetually looking over our shoulder at others. Someone will always be better in some areas; we can never be satisfied. The mirror of perfection will never be found as long as all we care about is keeping up with others. The reason for that is because we see *others* in our own mirrors.

My Dad had a favorite saying: "You can't win them all." He had learned that from his experience as a coach, but I didn't appreciate those words because they always came after my team lost a game.

Those words weren't consoling after a loss. They weren't the encouraging words I needed at the time.

Not that it made his saying wrong. Expectations to end up in first place are too high in our culture. Even the coaches who are great examples for our youth lose their jobs when they taste defeat too often. But first place isn't always what's best for God's people. We learn more from our losses and setbacks than wins and blessings.

Examples abound of parents who go beyond boundaries in pushing a child to win and to excel in performance. The high school senior whose athletic scholarship was axed by a division one coach because his parents constantly complained about their son's play, the coaching and the refereeing. The parent who beat up the coach of his son's little league team. The high school conference unable to find referees because of the parents' continual harping.

Consider a story Jesus told called the parable of the talents (Matthew 25:14–30). It's often been used to teach about stewardship but there is another valuable lesson here. The first steward was given five talents, and he immediately went right to work with them. When the master returned from his trip, this steward had doubled the master's money. The master then responded, "Well done, good and faithful servant. Enter into the joy of your master."

Similarly, the second steward was given two talents, and offered the master two more. Then the master could have said, "You didn't keep up with the first steward. He brought back five talents."

But no guilt was laid on this steward. No, the master's response was the very same to him as to the first steward: "Well done, good and faithful servant. Enter into the joy of your master."

The second steward was not concerned with keeping up with the first. He merely did his best with what he was given. You see, it's not the amount we're given that is the most important gift in life. It's what we do with the gift that is the biggest priority!

The second steward calls us to be content with all the blessings and all the gifts God gives us. Only here can perfectionists begin to find healing, for the pathway to healing starts with learning contentment and gratitude for blessings we receive. Yet it won't help the perfectionist one bit to work harder to accomplish any goal. It begins with the simple acceptance of the many positive gifts we have been handed.

The recipient who was given only one talent turned out to be the loser in the story. It wasn't because he received the least; it didn't bother the one who received two talents that he was handed less than the one with five talents. The steward with only one talent likely responded as many with few abilities do. "Oh, well, I have no talent. I won't even try."

Or he could have compared himself to the other two who received more talents in the story. Then his response could have sounded like this: "I got left out. I wasn't offered a deal anything close to what the other two got. So forget it! You think I'm going to bust my gut for nothing? I'll just bury my talent over here and worry about it later!" We get into trouble when we fall into the trap of comparing ourselves to others.

Although we've discussed the push parents give in this chapter, I want to offer encouragement to all who have the courage to take on the immense responsibility of parenthood. It's not easy.

Expectations from our culture make parenting even more of a challenge than it was in past generations. Today's society is not as easily influenced by Christian values than in the past. Children's sports activities occur on Sunday mornings when children once attended church in years past.

There is a whirlwind of activities luring children to participate. It costs more for most of those activities than it did in the past. For youth involved in sports outside school, recent studies estimate parents spend a total of $50,000 per child for entry fees, equipment, food, lodging, and transportation. Considering these and many other pressures on today's parents, they need to be supported with our prayers.

But parenting is also extremely rewarding. The greatest feeling in my world is the moment I return home after a meeting out of town or after a long day at work. When my daughters hear the automatic garage door going up, they rush to the back door and yell, "Daddy's home! Daddy's home!"

They bounce with excitement. They're happy to see me. I feel needed. I feel appreciated.

Going back to our neighbor, Mark couldn't have been happy years later with the sports accomplishments of his three daughters. They played some basketball in community college but they never arrived as sports stars. No full scholarships to four-year colleges. Two of them rehabbed from major knee surgeries. Two of them sat on the bench at a small four-year college. The daughters looked as if they weren't having any fun in sports but I was about to discover some younger kids who were.

CHAPTER THREE

Lower the Bar
(To a Height You Can Clear)

"Anything that's worth doing is worth doing badly."

—G. K. Chesterton

I have vivid memories of coaching both of our daughters and their teams in tee ball. Those teams included five- and six-year-old boys and girls. Attention span presents a challenge for this age. We led the league in dandelions picked in the outfield. We had players who would hit the ball and then run to third base. The highlight for most of the players was drinking the soda pop after the game. They hadn't learned to take it too seriously, and the ballplayers had fun on those teams.

On defense, it was a battle to teach them to run after the ball and throw it to first base. My instructions were clear: "If the ball is hit toward you, then run after it and throw it to first base." The next batter hit the ball to the pitcher's mound, and all ten of our players went after the ball. They made a dog pile ten players deep on the pitcher's mound. They were just following directions!

My experience as a baseball fanatic should have qualified me for the job as coach. I had faithfully studied the sports pages every day. Played hours and hours in youth baseball and slow pitch softball.

Had been well-schooled in the value of a vacuum sweeper defense. We baseball fanatics are wise to the fact that a pitcher's best friend is......... THE DOUBLE PLAY.

It doesn't seem all that complicated. Shortstop to second to first. How simple is that? It looks pretty easy when the pros turn two on TV.

Have you ever tried to teach five- and six-year-olds to complete a double play? The first challenge is for a player to field a grounder. Next, try teaching the shortstop or second baseman to cover the bag. Third, I said a prayer for the ball to find second base. Then, there is the hope the fielder on second base will catch it. Fifth, the next throw must find first base. And last, the first baseman must catch it. Only six actions must click for the double play to be completed. After practicing it for thirty minutes, we moved on to hitting off the tee and running the bases.

The fun was seeing how much progress the kids made. Rachel's team showed up for our last game with a record of 0-8. The team we played was 8-0. Their pitcher whooped it up in a pre-game celebration. "This will be no contest," he bragged.

He was right. Our team was highly motivated, and we won by a wide margin.

I was glad that by the time Andrea was playing tee ball, the officials had decided that we would not keep score. The only ones shading in the diamonds in the scorebook were some parents in the stands who just had to know who won. But the kids had more fun without the scorebook.

I can remember times when my Dad would be playing basketball with us—the score was tied—when we were informed that dinner was ready. Dad always said, "That's a good place to quit."

By then I was dead-set on winning the game. I said, "No way! Someone's got to win the game!" But Dad was teaching us that the game is for fun and exercise more than it is to designate a winner and a loser.

We never got a short-to-second-to-first double play. But we had a lot more fun, once my expectations were lowered. Perfectionists can enjoy life, if their expectations can be brought down a notch or two.

Clinical psychiatrist David Burns agrees in his book, *Feeling Good: The New Mood Therapy*. Chapter Fourteen—entitled "Dare to Be Average!"—contains the best coaching for a perfectionist I have found anywhere. Burns challenges the perfectionist to work at becoming average.[1] He points out that perfection will never be attained. On the other hand, to be average is something we can all strive for and achieve.

Dr. Burns offers fifteen suggestions for perfectionists. He first recommends making a list of advantages and disadvantages of being a perfectionist. He also advises us to try the following: "Choose any activity, and instead of aiming for 100 percent, try for 80 percent, 60 percent, or 40 percent."[2] It sounds ridiculous to us perfectionists, but it works!

I read essentially the same advice in a golf how-to book. If a golfer is hitting an iron to the green and tries to hit the ball too close to the pin, an errant shot is usually the result. If, however, the same golfer is content to simply hit the green, better shots follow. Similarly, when hitting a chip shot, aim for a three-foot radius around the cup; that will bring more success than trying to make the shot. Or with a long putt, be happy with coming within two feet of the cup. This takes the pressure off, helps us relax, and raises the success level.

His advice works for tennis, too; the percentages are better if we try to hit the ball within a foot of the corner than trying to be too fine and hit the corner. This type of thinking can be applied to about anything.

Perfectionists need to learn not to try too hard. The desire to do well causes the perfectionist to overfunction. How surprising that the results turn out better when we relax compared to when we try too hard! In coaching George Brett on hitting, Charley Lau's advice was, "Try easy, George."

When I used to lay down with six-year-old Rachel at night, she often had trouble getting to sleep. She said, "I'm trying, but I can't get to sleep."

My advice usually goes, "Try easy. Don't worry about getting to sleep. Relax."

Most nights, it works. Perfectionists can learn to try easy.

Burns has more valuable recommendations. We can compare by percentage how effectively we did an activity with how much satisfaction that activity gave us. We soon discover that some activities—though accomplished with great effectiveness—offer little satisfaction and vice versa. Burns also says it's almost impossible to find anything that can't be improved, so he encourages us to look at how things can be improved in our environment.

Baseball history provides a primary example. In 1941 Mickey Owen handled 476 chances during the regular season as catcher for the Brooklyn Dodgers without making a single error. On the other hand, Owen dropped the ball on the third strike in the seventh game of the World Series. It cost the Dodgers the World Championship. Owen admitted, "It was my fault."[3]

But it did not end his successful baseball career. And the success did not stop with baseball; he later served as County Sheriff in Greene County, Missouri for sixteen years. He was asked to run for Congress, but didn't want to travel again. For Mickey Owen the perfect season did not last, but one error in a big game did not devastate him either.

Burns suggests we confront the fear behind perfectionism. The perfectionist is asked to observe response prevention, a refusal to avoid pain. If we ever plan to overcome perfectionism, exposure to pain must be confronted. David Burns reminds perfectionists that it's never a good investment of our time when we spend hours looking for a lost item.

Failure in at least some of our goals is inevitable. Set process goals rather than results goals. Results are focused only on the bottom line, while process goals search for simple steps over which we do have control.

Productivity in our work can usually be increased if we strive for 80% percent efficiency instead of 100% percent. Burns gives the example of spending two years on his first academic paper.[4] In the same time, some of his colleagues had ten papers published. With less effort, he could have done the same.

Finally, he warns us not to lose our capacity to make mistakes because in so doing we also forfeit the opportunity for learning and growth.

I'll never forget the look on my stepfather's face when he saw my sophomore grade card. I had "A's" in chemistry and geometry, but a "D" in typing. His LOOK asked, "Did you come from Mars?"

Not much was said, but my mother took the bull by the horns, and soon Mom, the typing teacher, and I were meeting after school. The problem? Perfectionism. The grading scale allowed no more than one mistake per assignment to receive an "A."

Though blessed with ten uncoordinated digitals, I wanted an "A" on every assignment. Each time I made a second mistake—which was too often—I ripped the paper out of the typewriter and threw it in the trash. The result meant a lot of zeros in the teacher's grade book. I had never completed an assignment.

Mom quickly saw the solution. She said, "You are going to have to hand in some 'B' and 'C' papers."

By the end of the second semester, my typing grade was a "B," the first time that grade ever made me happy. For a perfectionist, the world doesn't end with a "B."

On God's grading scale, it wasn't a "B" or pass or fail. God's grading scale simply says, "He did his best."

We still do not end our quest for excellence in our work. We continue to do our best on any test or challenge. But it means we are more relaxed. We don't spend so much time fretting and stewing. We accomplish more by not overdoing it. Carl Jung says, "Fulfill something you are able to fulfill rather than run after what you will never achieve."[5]

Jesus reminds us that all the little things we tend to worry about have already been taken care of by our Heavenly Father (Matthew 6:25—34). We are advised to "seek first the kingdom of God and His righteousness and all these things will be given to you as well" (verse 33). Jesus is talking about food, drink, and clothes, but it's not out of context to mention the myriad of other little things we worry about. God has provided for our needs.

When Rachel and I shoot free throws, we do worse if we put added pressure on ourselves. We miss at times because we are trying too hard. When we relax, we have more fun. When we're having fun, we make more shots. We've set the bar too high. It's okay to lower the bar.

CHAPTER FOUR

Breaking up with Parental Control

"The real self is put back in charge when we can establish a relationship of equality with our parents."

—Karen Horney

Glenda and I had just listened to the parent-teacher conferences for our daughters. The sixth grader's teacher said, "Rachel is a perfectionist. She worries too much. She needs to relax."

I replied, "She comes by it honestly. She has two parents who are perfectionists."

We moved on to the conference for our first grader. The comments of Andrea's teacher weren't much different. "Andrea is a perfectionist and she worries."

Our family system offers evidence that standards of the parents are carried on in the children. Likewise, the family tree affects the pressure to strive for perfection. Rachel has to deal with four consecutive preceding generations of first-born ancestors in the genealogy, and the other side of the family includes such relatives as "oldest daughter" or "oldest living sibling" in some very large families.

Going back even further in the family history, we find more reason for tendencies toward perfectionism rooted in our past.

Seven ancestors arrived on the Mayflower in November of 1620; never mind the fact they were servants on the ship. More than likely, they brought a Puritan work ethic that pulled them toward perfectionism.

Referring back to birth order, it is a determining factor in how a child gravitates toward perfectionism. As implied above, the first-born is the most likely to end up a perfectionist. Parents regularly reward the first-born's driven, goal-oriented behavior. The oldest is the pickiest in the family, the one most difficult to satisfy. I am entitled to say that as the oldest child of six siblings.

Miriam Adderholdt-Elliot records three reasons the first-born is more apt to be geared toward perfectionism.[1] First, the parents are more insecure with no child-raising experience; therefore, they favor the thinking that they're doing a wonderful job of parenting if the child is a real go-getter. Second, the child spends more time with the parents, resulting in higher standards for the oldest. And third, the first child is more often a gifted child—who are more prone to perfectionism.

Kevin Leman confirms Adderholdt-Elliot's theories in his book, *The Birth Order Book: Why You Are the Way You Are.* Leman also says the first-born is seen for counseling the most frequently.[2] Statistics also show that the first-born is the most likely candidate to commit suicide.

Let's add a final reason the first-born has the curse of most likely to be a perfectionist. Since the youngest child is the smallest and most fragile, it's only natural for the parent to do everything to protect this child. As a result, the oldest feels some jealousy and a need to earn the parents' love. The need for the child to prove his or her worth to parents makes this child susceptible to perfectionism. At the same time, the possibility of perfectionism in younger children is not eliminated when the previously mentioned factors are present.

Both parents play a crucial role in handing down perfectionism to their children. David Stoop asked perfectionists to name other perfectionists in their family. 44% percent named the father only; 8% percent named the mother only. 32% percent listed both father and mother; 16% percent designated no one.[3] Those who named the father maintained the reason was his strong influence. Yet when the mother was said to be influential, she was perceived as competing with the father.[4]

Although these statistics point to the importance of the father's role, Stoop also stresses the value of the mothering role in the development of self. He holds that problems of perfectionism are a result of difficulties in this process in the development of the self.[5] It is also critical for *each* parent to have a sense of self in order to have the courage to set boundaries in relating to members of the family as persons. Affirmation is necessary, but so is setting boundaries.

Stoop has found four possible causes of perfectionism in the family setting.[6] Perfectionism grows by: (1) a spirit of criticism, (2) the observation of parents' expectations of themselves, (3) the setting of extremely high standards by the parents or significant others, and (4) a lack of standards set by the parents, and it is then up to the child to become the standard-setter.[7] This valuable input can guide us in looking for ways to be a positive influence as a parent.

Karen Horney focuses on a crucial time in the child's life we call the "terrible two's." She says that during that year a feeling of helplessness or anxiety blossoms whenever the child knows the parent is not present.[8] Horney lists three important aspects of this basic anxiety: (1) a feeling of isolation, (2) a sense of helplessness, and (3) a presence of hostility.[9] This is a critical age when the child needs the simple presence of the parent; without the parents' attention, the child develops a deep sense of rejection.

In a day when single parents—and married mothers and fathers, too—are forced to work long hours for economic reasons, it is not surprising that perfectionism has become prominent. There are many more occasions when parents are not available, making it critical for parents to set aside time to spend with their children.

Perfectionism develops within the child when the parent is preoccupied with other things. Possibly it's a workaholic parent who's never home. It could be a parent who is forced to moonlight for financial reasons. Or most painful for the child is the parent who is home a majority of the time, but refuses to hang up a cell phone, shut down the computer, or turn off the remote to the cable television. The child in that home is neglected, even though the parent is nearby.

In a counseling session, I listened to Harvey pour out the pain in his heart. He had gotten little attention from either parent. The message he remembered from his Dad said, "Son, I'm too busy. I have to work now."

His mother gained no attention from her husband either, so she escaped by spending all her time reading romance novels. With little attention from either parent, Harvey succumbed to perfectionism and compulsive eating. Harvey showed some progress in conquering both, but he also learned he had a life-time battle on his hands. His parents will never realize what damage they have done to their son nor will they have the opportunity to correct the damage.

Healing from perfectionism can never occur until the unconscious self is able to make a break from the parents. In referring to the mother-daughter relationship, Marion Woodman writes, "Unconscious identity is involved in power; one person is expecting another to live out her expectations. The child picks up the unconsciousness of the parent and carries that weight with her."[10]

Woodman then gives the example of a mother's fear of letting her child bake cookies. Mom is afraid of how the child's cookies will turn out, so the mother does it for her. Although the child is praised for her cookies, she knows they are not her work. Unconsciously, the more successful she is, the more she feels it is not really her, but her mother in her who is baking the cookies. Woodman says, "Her inner sense of failure is thus in direct proportion to her outer success."[11]

In another example, a church official welcomed the participants at a church workshop. She said, "My mother decided I'd play the piano. She planned on hearing me play the piano in church. I practiced with my parakeet on my hand. I never played in church."

In her own mind the child has to perform perfectly to be loved. Perfectionists strain to earn love by trying to live up to standards originally set by parents—not necessarily on a conscious level—but more likely on an unconscious level. Carol Van Klompenburg feels that we often mistakenly treat our families as extensions of ourselves, which blurs the boundaries of self.[12]

The unconscious tie described above is accompanied by a feeling of rejection toward the parent. Because it often results from an event that seemed traumatic to us, it plays over and over in our minds. This event may have been caused by extreme cruelty or it might have come from a time when the parent was simply tired, simply being human. Hasn't every child felt the parent too harsh, too authoritarian at some time? Because of this unconscious tie, we even feel guilty thinking of parents in these terms; the unconscious pedestal we put them on won't allow us to think of them as human. Yet we can't blame it all on the parents. James Jolliff had similar feelings when he confessed, "This is awful the way I keep incriminating my patients' poor parents."[13]

In order to see ourselves honestly, the unconscious identity with our parent must be shattered. Past feelings of rejection must be worked through in the unconscious. We can learn to say "No" when parents throw manipulation by guilt our way. We can work to relate to parents on an equal basis. If we do, we will gain an authentic image of who we are.

This process is called differentiation by those who employ family systems theory. Differentiation gives us the power to claim the self rather than giving in to the expectations and demands of others. It empowers us with the strength to be set free from parental control. It allows us to say "No" and set limits on what other persons may want from us. And it gives us the freedom to allow others to say "No" without manipulating them.

In preparing to officiate at a funeral, I was told by the lady whose father had passed away, "I never doubted that my father loved me."

If I hadn't known her well, I would have thought she was stretching the truth. But in every conversation with her, she had never failed to be honest with me. That strong statement indicated that she had passed through the process of differentiation. She had come to the place of feeling no rejection, knowing there was no unconscious hold on her from her father.

We can feel much better about ourselves when we look in the mirror, knowing that parental control is in the past.

CHAPTER FIVE

In Quest of a Mirror

"There is nothing wrong with enjoying looking at yourself in the mirror, … but it's important for every woman and man, I think, to really think for a few minutes about whether there is a point of diminishing returns. Because we have so much more to offer the world than just our looks."

—Kjerstin Gruys

On vacation, our daughters discovered mirrors like those at a state fair: a "House of Mirrors." Rachel and Andrea shrieked with laughter when they saw surprising new images of themselves. "I like this one; I'm very tall and thin."

"And this one cracks me up. I'm so short and fat."

"Look how big my head is!"

"Well, look how big my stomach is in this one!" Another roar of laughter.

Laughter is a healthy response. Some people might be offended, as if there's trouble dealing with the real image in the mirror. Let's focus on the first response above, the one saying how much she likes the view showing her tall and thin. That is what our society has come to expect, a theme we will discuss in more detail in the next chapter.

Most people delight in seeing some new options. They would love to choose the image they want from that shopping smorgasbord.

How wonderful life would be if we could actually look like the physical appearance we imagine for ourselves!

The perfectionist is like that. With damaged self-esteem, the perfectionist journeys through life looking for an appealing image. Endless streams of people look in every conceivable place for an image of self that will offer some small morsel of happiness. The perfectionist window-shops for a suitable image like most people search for new clothes. Perfectionists look from job to job, from counselor to counselor, even from marriage to marriage in the hope one of these will uncover an image of self that is tolerable. This search continues until the seeker is forced to confront the self and work through personal flaws, baggage, and esteem issues.

Unfortunately, the seeker is further shackled by the search itself. The accompanying perfectionism takes us farther away from the goal of personal healing and wholeness. The image we search for is further distorted by an unconscious perfectionism. The search for the ideal world continues.

For example, someone might say, "If only I can lose ten pounds, I will be happy."

Or another person may say, "If only I can get that promotion in my career, I will be content for life."

But when either goal is attained, the image appears no better. The standards simply go up. Why? The perfectionist automatically believes the goals were not set high enough at the outset. The perfectionist thinks, "Set the bar higher before I have time to be happy about clearing that last jump."

We will search for a mirror—an image of self—that will offer gradual contentment for unhappy perfectionists. We will also look at some deceptive mirrors of self and note how they distort the real image. We won't spend an inordinate amount of time looking in the mirror. Our goal, instead, is to find a mirror reflecting an image of self even a perfectionist can like. Our objective is to find a mirror that offers healing and wholeness to a perfectionist.

Perfectionists visualize an ideal world and try to live in it. It originates in the "terrible two's" when we try to cope with anxiety. Karen Horney maintains that this feeling of anxiety is founded upon an "all-pervading feeling of being isolated and helpless in a poten-tially hostile world."[1] Horney also holds that the child may not have to endure extreme circumstances to feel this anxiety, for even being hungry and crying in a crib can create it.[2]

In an effort to destroy these feelings of anxiety the child may overcompensate by visualizing the imperfections of the world as outside and perfection as part of the self. Althea Horner sees this idealizing of the self as a natural stage of development; at this time the child realizes its own helplessness and the mother's separateness.[3] Over time the imagination develops an idealized picture of the self. The ideal self copes with anxiety by living in an illusion different from the real world.

This idealist image is skillfully portrayed in a picture appearing in David Stoop's book, *Living with a Perfectionist*.[4] It depicts an obese woman looking in a mirror. The reflection she sees is an image of a slim attractive lady. The energy of the perfectionist becomes com-pletely directed toward the ideal self rather than the real self. This is the perfectionist's mirror of deception.

Another distortion in the mirror is the need for a perfectionist to be right all the time. It's hard to live with a person who, in his or her mind's eye, never makes one mistake. Or at least never admits making a mistake.

A scene at the end of the movie, "Butch Cassidy and the Sundance Kid," illustrates the perfectionist's reluctance to confess a mistake. The bank-robbing duo hightail it from America and arrive in Bolivia where they are chased into an open-air market. They are able to find cover there, but they are surrounded outside by a large posse of soldiers, all shooting bullets at them. As the gunfire rever-berates in the background, Butch says that they need to journey to Australia next. While they plan their next strategy, Butch says to Sundance, "I think it's only one guy."

Sundance holds up his cowboy hat and it is immediately blown away by many bullets. He says, "Don't you get sick of being right all the time?"

Those who associate with a perfectionist may get tired of trying to argue with someone who is "right all the time."

As we continue to search for a mirror, let's hear from one who refused to look in any mirror for one year. ABC News reports the story line of Kherstin Gruys, a twenty-nine-year-old PhD student, who was able to avoid looking in the mirror for one year.[5] Her plan originated from her struggles with body image and her experience in conquering an eating disorder. In high school, she was anorexic. She also read in a book, *Birth of Venus*, about nuns in Italy who had strict rules against vanity. "They didn't have mirrors in their lives,"[6] Gruys said.

"I just kind of kept coming back to this pattern of perfection-ism, and obsessing about my appearance, and I thought, iIf I can't think myself out of it, then maybe I need to change something about my environment to force me to change. The project was to get rid of the mirrors with the intention of focusing on everything else in my life,"[7] Gruys pointed out.

For many months, Gruys started her day by brushing her teeth, even though a curtain covered her mirror. She slipped her contacts in and put her makeup on by touch, not by sight. "The first month of the project... . . . when I was walking out the door... . . . it was maybe a 50-50 shot that I had mascara on my nose,"[8] As she drove to work, she looked in the rear view and side mirrors, but avoided looking at herself.

She learned to avoid eye contact with windows and other reflec-tions. She put faith in her friends to tell her what looked good in dressing rooms rather than using a mirror. And she put complete trust in her hair stylist.

"All my obsessing was kind of directed at how much I weighed," she said.[9]

She endured serious health problems from her anorexic pat-tern of limiting her intake of food and water. "I had kidney stones five times... . . . and the lack of body fat started affecting my bone density."[10]

Much to her mother's chagrin, Kjerstin continued her experi-ment throughout her engagement and wedding. She previously saw herself in the mirror and thought maybe she should lose some weight before the wedding. But that wouldn't work with her history of an eating disorder. She said the wedding day was actually pretty easy to get through without a mirror. "I'm getting my focus back to thinking about the real meaning of the day, which isn't how I look but marrying the love of my life,"[11] she said.

Appropriately, the first dance with her fiancée at the wedding was a song entitled, "You'll Be My Mirror." The lyrics sound out a fitting message; "I find it hard to believe you don't know/The beauty that you are."

The project finally reached its climax with a celebration surrounded by family and friends. Kjerstin Gruys peeked at her image at last. "I had a little ambivalence, and at the same time, pleasure, because I was happy with what I saw."[12]

It took years of therapy for Gruys to put her eating disorder in the rear-view mirror. But she reached out to others who were battling the same disorder by volunteering for About-Face, an organization based in San Francisco that helps those struggling with eating disorders.

Aubrey Toole was one of those who attended the party celebrating the end of Gruys's experiment. Toole is also a volunteer for About-Face. Toole said, "So many things are important about her message. I think so much of being a female in our society today is seeing yourself from the outside. And her message is really to see yourself from within."[13]

That message coincides with a passage in the Bible. God has asked Samuel, the prophet, to find Jesse's son, the honored son whom Samuel will anoint as king. The first son, Eliab, looked like the best prospect. As Samuel looked at Eliab, he said, "Surely this is the one!"

"But the Lord said to Samuel, 'Do not consider his appearance or his height, for I have rejected him. The Lord does not look at the things people look at. People look at the outward appearance, but the Lord looks at the heart'" (I Samuel 16:7). We humans want to judge by the outward appearance, but God has other priorities; He looks at the heart.

Our daughters found something to laugh about in the "House of Mirrors." Kjerstin Gruys felt mirrors are nothing to laugh at, but something she was compelled to run away from. Let us continue our search for a mirror we can trust, an image that will give us confidence.

CHAPTER SIX

The Mirror of Appearance

"Charm is deceptive, and beauty is fleeting, but
a woman who reveres the LORD is to be praised."
—King Lemuel's mother in Proverbs 31:30

Since Glenda was already on the road to work, it was up to me to prepare a nutritious breakfast before the girls went to school. A banana
nut muffin, heated in the microwave, sounded healthy.

Andrea was busy reading the label. "This muffin has fourteen
grams of fat!" she exclaimed. I was surprised that our daughter, only
six years old, was reading labels to check out how much fat she was
consuming.

But there are so many influences in our culture that point young
girls in that direction. The image of women as actresses in movies
and television, models in catalogues and nearly every picture we see
magnifies females who are young, thin, and beautiful. An unrealistic
pattern is unfolding in the young girl's mind for how she wants to
look. And our society ranks appearance as its number one priority.

Andrea loves to play with Barbie dolls. She dresses and undresses
different models of Skipper, Ken, and Barbie. She even has a Barbie
car that she can wheel around in our unfinished basement. In this
make-believe world, she is preparing for the adult world.

Notice Barbie's features. Thin arms and legs, narrow waist and
hips, oversized breasts, satin hair and perfect complexion. Have you

ever seen a Barbie with a birthmark? Barbie is thinner than TV models. She does not look like most women we see in the grocery store, the shopping malls, or on the job.

By spending hours with these Barbies, Andrea's expectations for how she will look as an adult have become fixated in her mind. As an adult, she will struggle with living up to these expectations. One recent study showed self-esteem for girls to be high at age eleven, but much lower by age seventeen. One major reason is unrealistic expectations for appearance.

In an article entitled, "Family Therapy for Bulimia," authors Richard Schwartz, Mary Jo Barrett, and George Saba discuss a disturbing trend: "constant pressure to dress fashionably, get good grades, make or marry into a lot of money and to look healthy and attractive (which means to look thin)."[1] Those pressures become a catalyst for the adolescent's self-esteem to nosedive.

The influence of the advertising media over our children begins at a very early age. At six, Andrea certainly hadn't heard us recite any specific number for grams of fat in any food.

Seeds for future anorexics are often sewn in a home with two parents who are goal-oriented, career-minded perfectionists. Symptoms of anorexia appear later during adolescence. They intensify during college years.

Who are the people suffering from eating disorders? A study revealed that 90 percent are women; 10 percent, men.[2] By 2012, the percentage of men had increased slightly to include one million men and seven million women in the United States. One study found that 25 percent of women in college have anorexia or bulimia. It is not surprising that the National College Health Assessment found that 26 percent of college women rated physical appearance as traumatic or very difficult to handle.[3]

Even more enlightening is the statistic that 91 percent of college women felt overwhelmed by all they had to do in the past twelve months.[4] 47 percent of college women felt hopeless about all they had to accomplish.[5] 87 percent felt exhausted, though not from physical activity.[6] An additional problem that accompanies eating disorders in college is sleep deprivation.[7]

The major factors in the onset of anorexia and bulimia are low self-esteem and a pattern of perfectionism. The person with an eating disorder perceives a need to have thoughts and behavior that are beyond criticism. When these goals are not met, a sense of failure and inadequacy follows. Cherry O'Neill, daughter of Pat Boone, battled anorexia. Her doctor, Raymond Vath, identifies other issues common for anorexics: sexual identity confusion, depression, power struggle, deception, dependency, and possible endocrine abnormalities.[8]

Because of denial and deception by the person with an eating disorder, it is virtually impossible for the family to make any progress toward healing. The one with the eating disorder will doggedly deny anything has gone awry in the relationship with the parents. Part of the appeal for the anorexic is that she feels in control when refusing to eat. Professional therapy is always urgent; death or long-term heart problems awaits those who refuse treatment.

Hilde Bruch suggests that the therapist gently guide the patient toward reconstruction of emotional interactions during the pre-illness period.[9] If this is the focus, the patient usually realizes the extent to which she has always done exactly what was expected, repressing her own self-determination. The absence of positive reinforcement and validation from the parent has cut off the development of self-esteem.

Marian Woodman defined the problem this way: "So long as her energy is going into that war with the complex, she has no energy to put into finding out who she is and what nourishment she needs."[10]

Yet there is a ray of hope; the anorexic usually wants a meaningful life. As Susie Orback says, "In every case of anorexia nervosa I have worked with, the woman has a great interest in having a life that is rich and meaningful."[11] Her withdrawal from this life that appeals to her comes from "…a fear that she will not measure up, that she is not good enough, and that she will not be accepted in the world of work or social contacts."[12] Orback lists other themes keenly felt by anorexic patients: "ambition, a desire to make one's mark in the world, a wish not to be confined or easily labeled."[13]

The anorexic is knotted up in a pattern of *doing* with no attention going to *being*. Disapproving parental images have become

37

internalized within the patient's mind, within her psyche. She bears the burden of knowing that nothing she has ever done could have brought happiness to her parents. Therefore, therapy needs to focus on rebuilding this individual while working through the pre-illness rejection.

The anorexic's mirror looks just the opposite of the picture we sawportrayed by David Stoops in the last chapter. When she looks in the mirror, she sees a picture of a person who is overweight, even though she has become so emaciated her appearance is frightening. Her likeness that she visualizes is exaggerated by many pounds, and her silhouette grows much wider than reality.

While eating disorders pose a danger mostly to women, a different addiction threatens men: pornography. Once again it is the advertisers who peddle their product by appealing to the male system that is stimulated by the visual image. Recent years have brought increasingly titillating commercials, not only suggestive and revealing of the female body, but also of the male. For the male who is into body worship, suggestive pictures abound on TV: aerobics, swimsuits, MTV. Magazine covers openly displayed in libraries and supermarkets have become more explicit. A man would have to be a hermit not to notice.

The lure of the suggestive frequently leads to a craving for the explicit. The desire for more explicit material grows. A further cause for the increase in the pornographic industry goes back to basic infancy needs not being met. At the time "baby boomers" were born, the baby was slapped and kept in the hospital nursery for a week. There was little bodily contact with either parent. Donald Joy contends that the bonding process was not allowed to take place.[14] Because of the lack of breast-feeding and bodily touch with parents, this particular generation has attempted to overcompensate. Generally, for women the result is eating disorders; for men, pornography.

As with other destructive addictions, the cause for pornography often goes back to emotional needs not being met in childhood, a vacuum vulnerable to any generation. Most addicts feel left out due to their fathers' failure to provide basic love needs. They feel a void. Most addicts to pornography will use some of the following terms about their fathers: workaholic, perfectionist, TV addict, withdrawn, not one to communicate, stone silent. When early needs for love are not met, in the male's visually-stimulated system, this converts to a need for visual love. The sex addict is deceived into believing the void where love should have been can be filled with sex.

In the last twenty years, the pornography industry has more than tripled, growing from an eight-billion-dollar industry to estimates of generating twenty-five to thirty billion dollars a year.[15] Every second, 28,258 internet users are viewing pornography.[16] Every second, $3,075.64 is being spent on pornography.[17] Some estimates go as high as 40% percent of American males have a problem with internet pornography. Among those in their teens, twenties, and thirties it is even higher.

Anyone hooked on pornography comes to worship the image of a perfect body instead of being able to relate to a real person as someone he actually loves. In the addicted person's mind, needs for intimacy can best be met by pornographic images. Relationships deteriorate. A recent news report said that men who regularly look at pornography were markedly less satisfied with their wives or significant others. In the addict's thinking expectations go ever higher; only the perfect body will do. Any image that is less than perfect amounts to a failure.

In a similar way, sexual performance can be wiped out by perfectionism. One study researching causes of impotence found perfectionism was a consistent factor.[18] Like other activities, when expectations shoot for perfection, disappointment follows.

Pornography distorts how we see ourselves in the mirror. The majority of those affected by it are men, even though the percentage of women who view it has gradually increased. Today it is more common for women to get involved through chat rooms.

Pornography stems from fathers who fail to give their children some necessary attention. It robs the viewer of self-esteem. Pornography wrecks relationships.

Another addiction, alcohol, distorts how we see ourselves in the mirror. It may not change our physical appearance, but it affects self-esteem and relationships in a destructive way. Alcohol and perfectionism are often linked, dependent upon one another. Dr. Prem Fry, Professor of Psychology at Trinity Western University in British Columbia, documents perfectionism as a cause for alcoholism.[19] One alcoholic admitted the reason for his drinking was a continuing failure to live up to perfection.[20] David Stoop says, "Some researchers believe that part of the reason the alcoholic drinks is to find serenity in a world where nothing is good enough."[21]

Once again, our young people are the target of the advertising industry. Three million alcoholics ages fourteen 14 through seventeen 17 point to the proof of the advertisers' "success."[22] While breweries spend exorbitant amounts on advertising, their commercials aim at a target group of males—ages eighteen through thirty-four—who drink 70% percent of the beer sold.

In contrast, positive role models have set out to change this commercialism. Dr. Jay Caldwell, director of the Alaska Sports Medicine Clinic, became incensed when the Alaska Midnight Sun Triathlon was renamed the Bud Light Triathlon. He wrote, "For blatant, and apparently acceptable, commercial exploitation of our youth by drug merchants, this even takes first prize…"[23]

Likewise, Bubba Smith quit the Miller Lite advertising team because of his convictions about the influence it had on young people. In an effort to emphasize positive role models, the country of Austria prohibits any public reference to alcoholic beverages. Dr. Klaus Leistner, director of the Austrian Ski Federation, says, "Sports and alcohol should never be placed together."[24]

Thirteen million alcoholics in this country could gain new life by practicing "Twelve Steps to Recovery" from Alcoholics Anonymous. These are steps from which those who are not alcoholic could also grow. The first step asks the addict to admit being a limited human being. Second, the alcoholic must confess an inability to handle the problem alone. Third, the alcoholic is requested to surrender control to God. These are the most difficult steps, but the most important.

The alcoholic devastates his family physically, mentally, emotionally, socially, and spiritually. Twenty-eight million "Adult Children of Alcoholics" live in this country. Because I lived with an alcoholic stepfather, I understand first-hand the perfectionism every family member develops in an alcoholic's home. I lived in fear of my stepfather going on another drinking binge. I did everything possible to strive for perfection; maybe that would stop the next drinking binge from occurring. Of course, I couldn't ever be quite that perfect! But in my mind, anything was worth a try to prevent another binge.

For the family of an alcoholic, life offers no stability. Nothing is predictable. There are no clues about what to expect. We didn't know when the next binge would hit. Family members try to be perfect for fear that if not, some small word or expression might set the alcoholic off on another drinking binge. Or it's easy to fall into the trap of believing the binge was my fault. Shame and false guilt always accompany that perception. And frustration is ever-present because the standards never stay the same in the home of an alcoholic.

When I was a senior in high school, I drove my brother, Dave, his date, and my date to a church-sponsored social. Soon after we arrived, my stepfather called and demanded, "Get your (selves) home."

Humiliated and frightened, I drove our dates home without explaining why. Then Dave and I went home. My stepfather ushered us before the fireplace and cracked our heads together. To this day, I don't know why. Another brother, Stan, later said, "Having your heads bounced together wasn't nearly as bad as wondering what would happen next." My experience is just one example of the destruction alcoholism leaves in its wake.

These three addictions—eating disorders, pornography, and alcohol—all affect the view in the mirror in a negative way. Considering these temptations for persons in the springtime of life, youth could use our prayer support in their battle against addictions. Marian Woodman attributes the source of addictions to a failure to meet spiritual needs. She writes, "Many people in our society are being driven to addictions because there is no collective container for their natural spiritual needs."[25] There are other damaging addictions that threaten—prescription drugs, sports, compulsive shopping, gambling—and the list keeps getting longer.

The grace of God offers hope to all who are hooked on destructive addictions. Each of us, through God's grace, can be transformed into a "new creation" through Jesus Christ. The Bible tells us that King Lemuel shared some words his mother taught him (Proverbs 31:1).

He wrote, "Charm is deceptive, and beauty is fleeting, but a woman who reveres the Lord is to be praised" (Proverbs 31:30). Consider that these words weren't spoken first by King Lemuel, but by his mother, a woman who likely had lived long enough to know that physical beauty was no longer a part of her reflection.

Our society values appearance as the highest priority, but King Lemuel's mother knew better. It's not as valuable as our culture claims. The mirror of appearance entices us toward a lifestyle that is overrated, as well as deceiving. Yet there are other mirrors besides appearance we need to see.

CHAPTER SEVEN

The Mirror of Performance

"You only have to bat a thousand in two things: flying and heart transplants. Everything else you can go 4 for 5."

—Beano Cook

Even though my Dad was a teacher and coach, he never once pressured me to perform in any sport. Although my Mom was usually in the stands to support me, she never coerced me toward sports immortality. At times, I wished that Dad would have taught me more of the fundamental techniques of sports. But I am grateful they let me set my own goals and didn't ruin my fun by expecting more than I could produce. Neither was ever overbearing about my performance in sports.

In contrast, the pressure on Olympic athletes must be unbearably heavy. It's exhausting to imagine, but Chinese gymnasts train sixteen hours a day. North Korea tries to motivate their Olympic athletes by promising them a new refrigerator for gold and hard manual labor for anything less. In the 2012 Olympics, North Korea won six medals, finishing tied for thirty-fourth among all countries. That method of enticement didn't bring great results!

On the other hand, American gymnasts train six hours a day, six days a week. American swimmers train five hours a day plus additional time for weight training. The athletes representing the United

States receive money for medals; how ironic since Jim Thorpe had his medals taken away after the 1912 Olympics for taking money to play baseball. Athletes from the United States earned 104 medals in the 2012 Olympics, sixteen more than the closest competitor, China. Less training, but the best results!

But when that much time is invested in training, the pressure to execute simply escalates. Add in pressure from coaches and parents, no matter how subtle. Worse, the whole world is watching on television. The competitors in women's gymnastics—or should I call them girls?—were only sixteen. One of them turned sixteen during the Olympics. Kids that age don't deserve to carry the weight of the entire globe when it comes to stress.

For example, Jordyn Wieber was favored to win the gold medal in the gymnastics all-around performance in the 2012 Olympics. The whole world watched as she didn't qualify for the finals. We also witnessed the tears in her eyes after she did not live up to the media's expectations or her own. My Dad might interject, "You can't win them all," but that wouldn't be any more consoling for Jordyn than it was for me.

Mark Lenzi felt the pressure in the 1992 Olympics, but was able to win a gold medal in the three-meter springboard for the USA. After attaining this lofty goal, diver Lenzi battled the depths of depression. He had pictured himself on the front of a cereal box, but that never happened. He expected to be at least a little famous, but that didn't take place either. Hardly anyone knew his name.

Two years after winning the gold, he was again in the pits. Even after he lived up to the expectations of others and his own goals, he found no fulfillment in the gold medal. He longed for competition and was in the doldrums. He called up his former coach, Dick Kimball, and asked if he would coach him again. In spite of Kimball's age of sixty-seven, he told Lenzi that if he was needed, he could still coach. Kimball was glad to be needed. Lenzi went on win a bronze in the 1996 Olympics in Atlanta.

Another pressure on both child and parent occurs when the parent overschedules the child. Before realizing how long the list of activities has become, the parent has the child enrolled in: music lessons, tee ball, gymnastics, dance, church Christmas program practice, swim lessons, library story hour, and on and on. The parent is racing to all of these before the child is in school. The result is what educational psychologists call "hothousing," stemming from the greenhouse effect of forcing plants to grow quicker.

Whew! The child is burdened with this whirlwind of activities! According to Miriam Adderholdt-Elliot, "Many psychologists believe that the Superkid Syndrome is creating a generation of children who are afraid to take risks and fearful of not getting the approval they have been raised to appreciate."[1] School principals and teachers agree that parental pressure to participate in more extracurricular activities has accelerated in recent years.

I must confess that we had Rachel and Andrea involved at an early age. Both daughters were taking gymnastics and dance by age two. Andrea tried to turn a cartwheel at that age, but it looked more like a basic donkey kick until she improved. At fourteen months, Rachel did not have to be pushed, but was happy to jump off the diving board for the swimming teacher. Their teachers made it fun and didn't push too hard.

A major part of the motivation in gymnastics was the trophy the girls were promised for completing a tumbling pass in good form. Rachel was thrilled when the instructor said she had finally done the aerial well enough to receive a trophy the following week. She was disappointed, however, when the trophy was not ready that next week. We had to wait another week, but that made it even more of a joy when it was presented. The trophy raised her motivation, but it can also add some pressure to perform.

In addition, we find pressure to perform in the classroom. Maria Pascucci is a "former frazzled perfectionist turned award-winning author, speaker, leader, and change-maker before her thirtieth birthday."[2] She is also the founder of Campus Calm. She had a 3.92 grade point average at Canisius College with a double major in English and history and a minor in writing. At the same time, she was working two part-time jobs. She says, "My resume was perfect, but I was a wreck."[3]

Her husband, Shawn, said to her, "I didn't marry your resume. I married you."[4] That's when she realized she needed to love herself from the inside first.

An earlier turning point came when she had a panic attack in the bathroom during a final exam. She writes, "I empower the next generation of rising women leaders—your daughters, students, nieces, and neighbors—to ditch their inner perfectionism so they can lead with resilience."[5]

You can check it out at _www.campuscalm.com_, an "award-winning online forum for today's stressed-out students, parents, and educators."[6]

We also feel pressure to perform on the job. Every job has some stressors and some expectations. I worked for three years as a sales representative for an office supply company. The boss promised a company car if I could reach his prescribed sales level four months in a row. It was as if he knew that it was possible three months in a row but not four. Each year December is a good month for sales, but February isn't. It fluctuates that way throughout all the months. I came so close, but the boss knew that sales were seasonal. Then there was the monthly quota. As soon as it was cleared, a higher quota was set.

We battle the pressure of performance, whether in sports, in academics, or on the job. The better the performance, the higher the expectations escalate. Likewise, advertisers sell their product by increasing our expectations to a level of perfection.

The advertising industry does not seem to live in the real world as it appeals to our need for perfection. They try to convince us that their product performs in a perfect way. Even the names of their companies on the internet point to the advertising ploy using perfection: Perfection Commercial Cleaning Services, Perfection Construction, Perfection Glass, even Perfection Pest Control. We also find: Sound Perfection, Perfection Building Maintenance, and Perfection Plumbing and Drain Cleaning who advertises a "passion 4 perfection." One automobile company airs its "Perfection" TV commercial, and another publicizes "the relentless pursuit of perfection."

Basketball player Kevin Durant appears in a shoe commercial, saying, "There is no such a thing as a perfect game of basketball." But by the end of the commercial Scottie Pippen is trying to convince us there is.

The advertising media is highly skilled at painting such appealing, appetizing pictures of food that our nasal senses are affected. Can't you just smell it? The power of suggestion makes us hungry! We are soon sold on the pizza piled high with cheese or a cheeseburger heaped with lettuce and tomato. David Stoop concludes, "Advertising is aimed at portraying the image of perfection. People buy according to this image, not according to reality—whether they can afford it or not, of course."[7]

I remember seeing a TV commercial for a big cheeseburger. The advertiser's mouth-watering picture would not let me forget it for a long week. And they were selling at half price! It wasn't only the perfect picture, but the price that hooked me, too. The simple power of suggestion had me thinking about that cheeseburger all week long. It became my major goal in life. I was willing to run over anything in the way of that cheeseburger. It's as bad as when I'm fasting and every other commercial on TV pictures fresh, mouth-watering food!

After a week of amazing discipline, I sped toward the nearest brand-name hamburger stand. At this bargain price, I better buy two. I hurriedly handed over the money and, in eager anticipation, jogged to the nearest booth. I chomped down, expecting it to taste just like the appetizing-looking one on TV. Funny thing, this one's cold. Tastes like it was stored in the bin for a week—probably the same week I've been craving it. How can it taste so awful? Where's that mouth-watering cheeseburger I saw in the commercial? The performance of the product isn't nearly as perfect as the picture!

A classic example of a home that would foster perfectionism is found in the movie, "Ordinary People." Cal Jarrett, played by Donald Sutherland, tries to be a compassionate husband and father; however, he devotes most all his time to his law practice. He doesn't schedule much time for his family.

His wife, Beth, played by Mary Tyler Moore, is preoccupied with her golf game and travel plans to Europe for Christmas. She is a perfectionist and favors the older son, Buck, because he performs better as a competitive swimmer than his brother. Buck's performance means everything to Beth, the perfectionist.

Conrad, played by Timothy Hutton, feels his mother blames him for the family tragedy of Buck's drowning. Dr. Berger, a psychologist played by Judd Hirsch, forces Conrad to deal with his guilt and previous suicide attempt. While the fall scenery is breathtaking, the portrayal of the Jarrett family is realistic but not quite as beautiful. Conditions in the home and the plot itself blend to point out contributing factors for perfectionism.

When it comes to performance, golfer Curtis Strange says, "We all choke. You're not human if you haven't." Since we've all failed, next we will discuss how failure can become our friend. But the mirror of performance is not the mirror we need.

CHAPTER EIGHT

Friendly Failures

"Failure is the opportunity to begin again more intelligently."

—Henry Ford

Every semester, I felt nausea in my stomach on the first day of college classes. That's when the professor handed out a massive syllabus listing all requirements for the course. Term papers, quizzes, major tests, daily reading assignments, reports, presentations, class or small group projects. It always sounded like a lot more than I could accomplish. Each thick synopsis of the course sparked my fear of failure. But over time—step by step, day by day—all those seemingly insurmountable tasks were transformed into valuable learning experiences.

Twice, Mickey Mantle came extremely close to ending his baseball career before it had gotten off to a good start. The first time, he had just signed with the Yankees and was farmed out to their lowest minor league team; he was playing for the Class D team in Independence, Kansas. Mantle called his father and told him he was ready to quit baseball. Mutt Mantle drove seventy miles from his home in Commerce, Oklahoma and convinced his son to continue playing baseball.

The second time, after being moved up to the Yankees' major league team in 1951, Mantle endured a terrible slump. The Yankees sent him down to their highest minor league team, the Kansas City

49

Blues. There he couldn't hit the long ball; his power seemed to be gone. He called his Dad and said, "I don't think I can play baseball anymore."[1]

Mutt Mantle drove 165 miles to Kansas City that day. Mickey Mantle said his father started packing Mickey's clothes and said, "I thought I raised a man. I see I raised a coward instead. You can come back to Oklahoma and work the mines with me."[2]

In a short time, Mickey Mantle was hitting with power again. He was called back up to New York after forty games in Kansas City. But he had wanted to give up baseball. Mantle twice got to the place he was feeling a fear of failure.

I see another father sitting in the stands, watching his son during high school football practice. Dad envisions his son playing in the NFL, making millions. Dad dreams of a new house, a new car, and his son providing for him in his old age. This father suddenly screams at his son, "Don't you know how to block? What's wrong with you?"

The son had been publicly humiliated, but more damage had been done. The seeds have been planted in the son's mind. Dad's message to his son is that he is failing at football. With no positive reinforcement, the son has a steep hill to climb in order to succeed. It's natural for the son to feel like a failure. UCLA Coach John Wooden said, "Young people need models, not critics."[3]

Fear of failure is a common trait of perfectionists. Since perfectionists are usually people pleasers, that fear of failure springs from a fear of criticism. Deep down, the perfectionist wants everyone to be happy. When one mistake can ruin the perfectionist's entire frame of mind, fear of failure skyrockets.

Aaron Beck was the first to point out that perfectionists maximize failures and minimize successes.[4] I know what he means! During a softball game I got two solid hits and made one out on a fly to the outfield. What did I remember? What kept replaying in my mind? The out! I was maximizing the failure and minimizing the successes.

When the perfectionist hears five compliments and one harsh criticism, he or she is going to remember the criticism much longer than the compliments.

A similar symptom is that of clinging to past mistakes.

Even though the apostle, Paul, is speaking of former accomplishments, his words of "forgetting what lies behind and straining forward to what lies ahead" (Philippians 3:13c) are appropriate for the perfectionist. Constantly looking in the rear-view mirror and asking, "Why didn't I perform better?" helps no one. Remembering a mistake once is enough. Learn from the mistake, thank God for the resulting lesson, and go on.

Inventor Thomas Edison had no fear of making a mistake. After three months in school, his teacher, the Reverend Engle, called him "addled."[5] Engle found Edison to be confused. Then Edison dropped out of school, and his mother taught him at home. His education was supplemented by learning about the telegraph from a train station master who rewarded Edison for rescuing the station master's three-year-old son from being hit by a train.

In attempting to invent the light bulb, Thomas Edison had trouble finding the best substance for the filament. He experimented with over 1,600 components before hitting upon carbonized bamboo as the perfect filament. He wrote over 40,000 pages of notes before he found a light bulb that would last forty hours. Finally, on September 4, 1882, Edison's Pearl Street station in New York City conducted electricity to lights in twenty-five buildings.

Thomas Edison said, "If I find 10,000 ways something won't work, I haven't failed. I am not discouraged, because every wrong attempt discarded is a step forward."[6]

Edison was close friends with Henry Ford and Harvey Firestone, who all succeeded because of the same outlook: mistakes simply open the door to opportunity and eliminate ways that won't work.

At the age of sixty-seven, Edison, along with his son, watched as his laboratory and factory burn to the ground. Thomas Edison responded, "There's value in disaster. All our mistakes are burned up. Thank God, we can start anew."[7] Edison welcomed mistakes, even when they seemed like failure.

Likewise, golfer Walter Hagen learned to enjoy his mistakes. Sportswriter Grantland Rice had a great appreciation for Hagen's sound philosophy of golf that Hagen applied to his game.

Hagen said, "Grant, I expect to make at least seven mistakes each round. Therefore, when I make a bad shot I don't worry about it. It's just one of the seven."[8]

Rice went on to say that he saw Hagen make nineteen mistakes in one round in a North and South Open at Pinehurst in 1924. Rice writes, "He finished with a 71, ultimately winning the tournament. A mistake meant nothing to him. Neither did defeat."[9]

Hagen irritated fellow competitor Bobby Jones who lost to Hagen in a 72-hole "World Championship" match. After that loss Jones said, "When a man misses his drive, and then misses his second shot, and then wins the hole with a birdie, it gets my goat."[10]

Walter Hagen and Thomas Edison offer us essential lessons in dealing with mistakes.

Fear of failure can become too drastic, threatening many who develop a phobia called atychiphobia. This extreme mental anxiety makes one irrational and afraid to try any risk without a 100 percent guarantee of success. Anyone with atychiphobia refuses to take any chances. This phobia affecting 2.4 million Americans causes physical illness including digestive problems, headaches, muscle tension, and panic. These panic attacks cause rapid breathing, dry mouth, sweating, and nausea. There is no complete cure, but counseling that includes cognitive behavioral therapy will help immensely.

At the first college I attended, economics class got the best of me. The professor was from China; though not his fault, I could not understand his English. This economics class was a second-level class and should have required a basic introductory class. The text book was all theory, and I was looking for something practical. By semester's end, I had failed the class.

After I enrolled at another university, my advisor looked at my transcript and steered me toward taking another economics class to eliminate the "F" on the grade point average. The professor in this economics class was an African American, very down-to-earth, practical and clear in his teaching. He joked with us students and cared about us in such a warm way. I loved his class.

When I got the highest score on the first test, he recognized me before the class. On the second test I had slipped to a "C." He didn't back down on the opportunity to razz me a little. In front of the class, he said, "I see you're resting on your laurels."

That comment had me motivated for the final. I later felt jubilation in knowing that an "F" on my transcript was now an "A." But it would have never happened without a professor who made me feel special.

In another case, I had a severe case of senioritis. I was nearly through seminary and had planned my classes so that my load of class hours was minimal for the last semester. Frankly, it was tempting to coast in toward graduation. The professor in one of my classes had led my small group through all three years of seminary. I had eaten lunch or breakfast with him every week for three years. He was not only my professor, but my friend. When he noticed I had turned in only a handful of homework assignments, he said, "You are winding down to disaster."

He too got me motivated with that comment!

Four Star General and former Secretary of State Colin Powell says, "There are no secrets to success. It is the result of preparation, hard work, and learning from failure."[11]

Consider an inspiring story—with 1.4 million Facebook hits—about Matt Woodrum, an eleven-year-old from central Ohio.[12] Matt was born three months premature as a twin. The doctor said Matt would live his entire life in a wheel chair as a vegetable. The doctor advised the family to take him off life support and let him go. But his mother said that was never considered. At the age of two, Matt was diagnosed with cerebral palsy that affected the left side of his body and made walking difficult.

Years later, when the school track meet came around, Matt decided he wanted to run the longest race: 400 meters. Matt claimed his physical education teacher, John Blaine, as one of his best friends for the previous five years. Mr. Blaine said, "There's no telling Matt he can't do anything."

The morning of the race Mr. Blaine was concerned and asked, "Can his legs handle this?"

Matt said, "I was nervous. I knew the race was long, but I wanted to start and finish, no matter how much it hurts."

Matt started running the race but in a short time, Mr. Blaine could see that he was starting to get tired. He said to Matt, "You aren't going to quit, are you?"

"No way."

His classmates were cheering in unison, "Let's go, Matt." Matt slowed down many times, but the cheering just got louder.

Mr. Blaine said, "He didn't stop running. He was going on adrenalin with all that cheering for him."

Matt got within ten meters of the finish line and said, "I've got to pass that finish line." When he crossed the finish line, Matt Woodrum heard the cheers of his classmates.

Matt added, "Just because I'm handicapped doesn't mean I can't do it. Cerebral palsy isn't going to slow me down."

Mr. Blaine said, "I got to witness something most people don't. He proved he can do what he sets out to do."

Blaine added a significant conclusion to Matt's story. "He wasn't afraid to fail."

Remember Matt Woodrum the next time you hesitate about taking a risk. Part of the healing for perfectionists occurs when we are willing to venture into deeper waters.

C. S. Lewis said, "Failures are finger posts on the road to achievement."[13]

It's likely you've read about the failures of our sixteenth President of the United States. In 1831 Abraham Lincoln failed in business. One year later, he failed by losing an election to the state legislature. In 1833 he again failed in business. In 1835 his sweetheart, Anne Rutledge, died. Though not formally engaged, they had a close relationship. One year later, he suffered a nervous breakdown. In 1838 Lincoln lost a bid to become speaker of the Illinois House of Representatives. He was defeated in becoming an elector in 1840. Three years later, Lincoln failed to receive a nomination for Congress.

He lost a second try to be nominated to Congress in 1848. The next year, Lincoln declined an appointment to be secretary, then governor, of the Oregon territory. In 1854 he failed in an effort to be elected to the United States Senate. Two years later, he failed to gain a nomination for Vice President of the United States. In 1858 he was again defeated from being elected to the United States Senate.

After all these failures, in 1860 Lincoln was elected President.

But he still had many difficult days ahead. In 1862, his eleven-year-old son, Willie, passed away. The casualties and battles of the Civil War weighed heavily on Lincoln's heart. Frequently, he prayed to God for help in his struggle. Yet failure never stopped him.

After his election as President in 1860 and before he actually lived in the White House, Abraham Lincoln continued to work at his office in Illinois. Late one afternoon, Lincoln went to his office for some rest. He lay down on the sofa to relax. Looking across the room, he could see his reflection in the mirror. Out of the blue, his image in the mirror changed. He could see two distinct images of his body. He got up and walked over to the mirror. The two images disappeared.

The president-elect lay down again, only to be shocked by the double images in the mirror. For the second time, he saw two different images of himself in the mirror. One face was full of life; the other was ashen and pale like death. He did not understand it, but later related the two images to his wife, Mary. The vision was clear to Mary; he would live through the first term in office, but die in the second. That vision haunted Lincoln. He said that every time it came into his mind, it "gave me a little pang."[14]

Though the vision troubled him, Lincoln forged ahead with courage. We may not like the image in the mirror, but we can learn from failures and overcome them. Failures are friendlier than they look.

CHAPTER NINE

Last-Minute Dangers

"Procrastination is one of the most common and deadliest of diseases and its toll on success and happiness is deadly."

—Wayne Dyer

My professor of Greek assigned us seminary students a word study. I chose *aletheia,* a word meaning "truth." I spent hours in research, spread out over two weeks. The night before it was due, I stocked up on Pepsi to keep me awake and then typed through the night. But by sunrise, it still wasn't completed.

The next day, I went to classes, drove the school bus route both morning and afternoon, and went to basketball practice. So once again the next evening, I got out the Pepsi, typed through the night, and finished that monster paper about sunrise. I was overjoyed to be able to hand it to the professor the first thing that morning!

I drove the school bus the next day after going forty-eight hours without sleep. God had to employ many more troops of guardian angels to protect the children on the school bus that day. I hope their parents aren't reading this!

The professor of Greek docked me a letter grade since the paper was a day late. He had asked us to write at the end of the paper how many hours we had spent in research and how many hours we had taken to write it. I wrote 35 and 35. He put a big red question mark beside those numbers.

The culprit? Procrastination. It usually accompanies perfectionism. The perfectionist procrastinates because of—what we looked at in the last chapter—a fear of failure. Procrastination is the perfectionist's effort to delay failure. Since the pressure to be perfect increases with any deadline, the perfectionist always postpones the venture to start the project. Then there is always a handy, catch-all excuse: how could I do a perfect job if I didn't have time?

The perfectionist also procrastinates because of a need to make things perfect. The perfectionist has a knack for a long, drawn-out agonizing over decision-making. That procrastination stems from a fear of making a mistake, a fear of hurting another person, and a polarizing black-and-white outlook. If you take an inventory survey and end up marking more "always" answers or "never" answers than anything in between, that would indicate a tendency to see things in black and white.

Glenda begins packing for a long trip months ahead of time. On the other hand, I wait until the day before. She says she won't forget to put everything in the suitcase if she starts months in advance. She doesn't forget as many items in her suitcase as I do, but she's been saved a few times when I packed an extra coat for her.

Perfectionists can fit any job into the art of procrastination. There are so many jobs we can put off. Clearing off my desk. Confronting an insensitive co-worker. Planning for retirement. Sending out a resume. Making out a will. Cleaning house. Changing the oil.

Procrastination steals our time. Henry Wheeler Shaw writes, "The greatest thief this world has ever produced is procrastination, and he is still at large."[1] Aaron Beck writes about taking two years to finish his first academic paper. In that same time period his colleagues had ten papers published. He undoubtedly was in a mode of procrastination. What could he have accomplished with that extra time? When I was working on my doctorate, we students joked about how creative we could be in procrastinating on our writing projects.

Procrastination can also be a warning signal. It may mean we are trying to cope with too much stress. It could mean we have too much on our plates. Ben Franklin tried to structure his day so that it included one-third work, one-third play, and one-third rest. We may need more time for play and rest. I carry a tiny super ball in my pants pocket. When stress heats up, I reach in my pocket and bounce it on the floor a few times. It reminds me of play from my childhood and lifts my spirit. I keep a golf putter in my office and set up a miniature golf course with a glass jar for the cup.

Procrastinators have quite the imagination when it comes to finding ways to avoid the task at hand. We spend time on trivial activities. TV is a great time-killer. Yahoo always has an interesting news flash on the net. Checking e-mail messages can fill our time. How many e-mail messages are not worth reading? Of course, we have to read through them to find out which are worthwhile. But no one is making us check them often or read every one. Or computer games steal our time.

For the perfectionist, the hardest part of any project is getting started. We can dream up a multitude of mental excuses for never buckling down on a project. We often put more energy into avoiding a task than it would take to accomplish it. All the emotional energy is going into escaping the job. For small projects, seventy-five percent of completing it is getting started. Olin Miller says, "If you want to make an easy job seem hard, just keep putting off doing it."[2]

I kept delaying a writing project because of what seemed like a lack of material. I kept procrastinating. Once I decided to list all the components of the article, I had too many building blocks! I felt awful that I had wasted so many hours in procrastinating.

Sometimes the "to-do" list seems too long, and we feel snowed under. Or the task at hand seems too large to accomplish. That's when it helps to break it down to smaller jobs. Mark Twain understood that; he said, "The secret of getting ahead is getting started. The secret of getting started is breaking your complex overwhelming tasks into small manageable tasks, and then starting on the first one."[3]

To get to the point of getting started, I like Steve Pavlina's idea of time-boxing.[4] He says to commit to thirty minutes at a job you don't want to do, and promise yourself a reward. Sometimes we desire to go longer. We often discover the job wasn't nearly as hard as anticipated. James Michener says, "Don't put off for tomorrow what you can do today because if you enjoy it today, you can do it again tomorrow."[5]

As an example, I used to run marathons. When first starting, I logged how many miles I ran. But a goal of running enough miles to run around the world was an afterthought. When I learned I always ran over a thousand miles a year, it seemed possible to run around the world. It would take twenty-five years to complete the goal at that pace. That was divided out to average 2 ¾ miles per day, a short distance compared to what I was used to running. I realized that goal was certainly attainable, and it was conquered. Then I found new goals by making it a triathlon; I walked around the world twice and bicycled around the world twice. But any major job can be broken down to several smaller tasks.

We may feel we don't have the skills to complete a large goal. Most skills take a major time slot for practice, so we keep prolonging the agony. When I was a Boy Scout, the Scoutmaster asked me to be the bugler for the troop. We had a Scout meeting, and they asked me to play "Reveille." I hadn't practiced; the result was my performance was so dreadful that no one could recognize the song. What an awful embarrassment!

During the next week, I spent hours of practice on the bugle. Again I played "Reveille" at our troop meeting the next week. Everyone in the troop couldn't believe it was the same bugler playing. A great improvement occurred in a week's time.

We may need other skills to overcome a big job. We might need to learn more in class to finish off a task. We may need to hand off part of the job to someone else. Sometimes I ask others at my work to take on a portion of a job. At other times, I'm joyously surprised when they've volunteered to do the job without even being asked. Sometimes we may be able to get rid of the job altogether.

Today I had on my list to repair the LED sign; one side was black without lighting up at all. Later I was driving by and noticed that both sides were flashing a message. Our custodian had turned the switch off twice and back on, and it was working again. There was great joy in scratching that off the "to-do" list!

Procrastination may be caused by work issues. Ask yourself, "Do I still have a passion for my work?" If not, it could be time for a change in employment. Our effectiveness quickly nosedives after working more than forty-five hours in a week. If your employer is expecting more than that, it may be time to send out your resume. Or if possible, schedule more down time.

Procrastination occurs more frequently when we are tired. Those trivial tasks we discussed are more inviting when our bodies are alert and rested physically. Maybe you are not sleeping enough hours. Or you might not be exercising enough to make you sleep. I sleep much better if I've been able to find the hours in the day to ride the bicycle a long distance. It could be that you are eating too much fat and not enough vegetables and fruit. Excellent physical health can indirectly keep us from procrastinating.

Elizabeth Kubler-Ross discovered those who had been through "near death" experiences made some major life changes. One was to live life to the fullest with less procrastination. She says, "It is only when we truly know and understand that we have a limited time on earth—and that we have no way of knowing when our time is up—that we begin to live each day to the fullest, as if it was the only one we had."[6]

Chuck Swindoll tells us to stop stalling. He says, "The habit of always putting off an experience until you can afford it, or until the time is right, or until you know how to do it is one of the greatest burglars of joy. Be deliberate, but once you've made up your mind—jump in."[7]

Stop waiting for the perfect moment; it never comes. It's all right to be human, so there is no need to fear failure. You'll learn a lot from a mistake, and the stoplight isn't going to turn a darker shade of green. Waiting is simply a waste of time.

CHAPTER TEN

Side Effects

"I cannot give you the formula for success, but
I can give you the formula for failure, which is,:
"'Try to please everybody.'"

—Herbert B. Swope

A medical doctor unloaded the pain in his heart to me. Jason said, "Even if there weren't laws about confidentiality, I'd respect my patients and keep their words quiet. I've shared my struggles with my wife, but she's leaked confidential information to other people when she should have kept quiet. The other doctors are too busy seeing patients, so I have no one to talk to.

"I have no idea where I'll be next. I could be delivering a baby in the middle of the night, trying to revive a senior citizen with CPR, ordering tests, or prescribing meds in the office. I might be questioning a patient just to come up with a diagnosis.

"And I can't go to the grocery store without being asked about someone's condition or the way to fix it. It's the same at my kid's school or church.

"They also expect me to have all the answers. They expect answers before the test results are back. People expect way too much. There's no way anyone could live up to all those expectations.

"I never know what it's like to have time to do the things I want to. If I get away, they'll track me down from the office and ask about the condition of a patient or to renew a prescription. Yeah, there's another doctor on call, but he's not going to know the history of the patient. I'm always working on my day off.

"And you wouldn't believe the demands on my time when I'm in the office. It seems like more than one person can do."

You've probably never heard your doctor talk like Jason because there is a public image to maintain. It may come as a surprise, but the doctor is human like the rest of us. Yet anyone in a profession serving the public—including the clerk in city hall, health care professionals, teachers, police, coaches, counselors, pastors, and several more—faces similar issues. Judging from his words and other verifiable symptoms discussed below, Jason is suffering from depression.

Perfectionists are more susceptible to depression than those who are not perfectionists. In a study that appeared in the *Journal of the American Psychological Association*, Doctor Kenneth Rice, Psychology Professor at the University of Florida, found that tendencies toward perfectionism become a risk factor for depression.[1] He also found that even after treatment and healing, depressed patients continued to be at risk to go through depression again. He says, "We don't just need to attend to their mood—we also need to attend to their personality."[2] Children rated by their parents as depressed on the Personality Inventory for Children were also found to be perfectionists.[3]

Depression is so common that 50 percent surveyed said that either they or their family members have suffered from it. 46 percent considered it a health problem. Dr. Stephen Ilardi, associate professor of clinical psychology at the University of Kansas, says that one out of four Americans will suffer from major depression sometime during their lifetime.[4]

The depressed person shows many side effects of the illness. Problems getting enough sleep plague anyone with depression. That causes fatigue and a lack of energy. There is an inability to focus and a lengthy pause as the depressed person stews over making decisions. The appetite either shrinks with a resulting weight loss or hunger increases, causing a weight gain.

Chronic pain or digestive issues persist. A sense of sadness pervades the depressed person's mood. The blues hit. Depressed persons feel a loss of enjoyment in activities that previously cheered them up. Feelings of guilt, hopelessness, and worthlessness grow. Thoughts of suicide may occur more frequently.

Stress serves as a catalyst for bringing about depression. It could be that the patient's job description climbs way beyond what's in black-and-white, and too often unwritten expectations are added on. It could be a death in the family or a relationship gone sour. It might be an illness or abuse, whether physical, verbal, or sexual. The stress can be passed down through heredity, passed down by parents or grandparents. It's often from isolation and loneliness. That's no farther away than the nearest nursing home, where the staff has no time to care for the patient. Medical staff are too involved with a multitude of medical reports to punch into the computer, doctor's orders to implement, and medications to administer.

So how can we overcome depression? Stephen Ilardi promotes a six-step program that will help without relying upon drugs. He recommends a diet rich in Omega-3, lots of intense physical exercise, and at least seven to eight hours of sleep. He further stresses making social connections, plenty of natural sunlight each day, and meaningful activity in serving others.[5]

It is again important to highlight the cure of cognitive behavioral therapy from a licensed professional counselor. A friend of mine who is a single pastor said that when she's feeling down, she pops the video of "Fiddler on the Roof" into the DVD player. Her blues are gone by the time the movie is over. "The Sound of Music" lifts my spirit. For our daughters, it was always "Annie."

Reading the Psalms can lift us in spirit. The Psalms of Lament remind us that David certainly felt some powerful emotions in a negative way. His words overflow with emotion; he too surely fought through some depression. But David also bubbled over with glee; his exhilaration is evident in his Psalms of Praise. For every Psalm of Lament we read, we can be encouraged by reading at least one Psalm of Praise. On the next page is a list in each category to help you out of the doldrums. All these Psalms are a love letter from God—the One who wants to cheer us up. Notice that 48 Psalms of Lament are on the list and 53 Psalms of Praise to give us encouragement. It's just like God to equip us with more celebrations than downers.

PSALMS OF LAMENT

Laments of the Community—12, 44, 58, 60, 74, 77, 79, 80, 83, 90, 94, 106, 123, 137

Laments of the Individual
General—3, 5, 6, 13, 22, 25, 28, 31, 39, 42--43, 52, 54, 55, 56, 57, 61, 63, 64, 71, 86, 88, 120, 141, 142

Protests of Innocence—7, 17, 26, 27, 59

Curses upon Enemies—35, 59, 69, 70, 109, 137, 140

Prayers of Repentance—6, 32, 38, 51, 102, 130, 143

PSALMS OF PRAISE

General—100, 113, 117, 145, 150

Praise to the Lord of Creation—8, 19:1--6, 29, 104

Praise to the Lord of History
The Mighty Acts of God—68, 78, 105, 106, 111, 114, 149

The Kingship of God—47, 93, 96, 97, 98, 99

Messianic (Kingship of Christ)—2, 18, 20, 21, 45, 61, 63, 72, 89, 101, 110, 132, 144

Praise to the Lord of Creation & History—33, 65, 103, 115, 135, 136, 146, 147, 148

Praise to the Lord of Zion
General—46, 48, 76, 87
Pilgrim Songs—84, 122, 134
Admission to Zion—15, 24

Journaling also offers a healthy outlet as we traipse through depression. Like David's Psalms, journaling allows us to be honest when we are in the pits of depression and when we are in the mountaintops of joy. It will help us to see patterns that develop in cycles as we journey through days, weeks, months, and years. It will assist us in seeing our progress over a period of time. Journaling helps us to see God working in our lives when we can look back and say, "Yes, God had a reason for that." Sometimes it is hard to see that reason in the present moment, but when we look back we understand that "in all things God works for the good of those who love Him" (Romans 8:28).

Another symptom is that perfectionists seldom say "No" to any new project. For example, I listened to a city mayor publicly thank a medical doctor for her commitment to helping penniless clients. The mayor said, "She doesn't know how *not* to give her all." It was intended as a great compliment; the audience took it that way. Yet this compliment made me wonder if the doctor was able to set limits, able to say no when necessary. Thomas Kelly understands the real issue; he says, "Much of our acceptance of multitudes of obligations is due to our inability to say no."[6]

I know people who never say no to serving on any committee or board. "No" just isn't in their vocabulary. They are flattered when asked to take leadership positions on any task force. Invariably, they end up overcommitted and overscheduled. Without even realizing it, they may find themselves hooked by a new beatitude in our busy, keep-on-grinding culture: "Blessed are those who run around in circles, for they shall be known as big wheels." Sometimes only a heart attack slows them down—and they don't understand why.

If you listen closely to a perfectionist, the word, "should," will crop up often. These "shoulds"—as well as the "should nots"—become like the boss. They rule over a perfectionist. "Shoulds" can possibly be only feelings that have not surfaced. Again, CBT (cognitive behavioral therapy) will help us get in touch with internal communications and prevail over the "'shoulds."

All-or-nothing thinking is another side effect of perfectionism. Everything is viewed as black or white; there are no shades of gray. One is either right or wrong; there is no in-between or compromise for the complex issues in life. This thinking in extremes is called polarization. It leads to the hurdle effect: a fear of trying any challenge because of the possibility of failure.

As an example, Dan O'Brien trained long hours for the decathlon in an effort to represent the United States in the 1992 Olympics. In the competition to qualify, he was on pace to score a record number of points. When the decathlon event got to the pole vault, he passed on heights he could have made. When O'Brien finally decided to vault, the bar was high enough that he missed three times. In the pole vault he received no points and failed to qualify for the Olympics. Just a few points at a lower height would have helped him to qualify. Maybe he was saving his energy for the other events in the ten-event competition. There likely were other factors in his decision, but this illustrates how the perfectionist thinks. It's usually all-or-nothing.

Another hurdle for the perfectionist is the trap of falling into a dead end of self-pity. The pitfall before us is a mind-set of constantly feeling sorry for ourselves. We can let God teach us gratitude as we see the unfortunate circumstances of others.

Our daughters' elementary principal, Willy Penner, had a traumatic childhood. A refugee in Poland after World War II, he didn't see his father from the time he was seven until age eleven and only occasionally saw his mother. He worked for a farmer and survived on a diet of potatoes. Willy didn't own a shirt, but borrowed one to have his picture taken. His hair was cut short, because when it grew, the lice had to be scraped off. He never attended school during those years. When he was thirteen, the family was reunited and immigrated to the United States. Willy started kindergarten in America at the age of thirteen without understanding a word of English!

Or consider the Jucan family who defected from Romania during the Communist reign of Nicolae Ceausescu. Husband Anca had a college degree in chemistry and agronomy. Wife Florentine had a college education to work as a pharmacist. Only 5 percent of the population in Romania had earned a college degree. And the bloodthirsty Ceausescu was sending many college graduates to the firing squad.

Florentine's brother had been the coach for the Olympic shooting team in Romania. He had defected to the United States and coached the American shooting team in Colorado Springs. After filling out many applications to visit and enduring loads of red tape, the Jucans were finally given clearance to visit Florentine's brother in Colorado Springs.

The family defected and settled in Sublette, a small town in the flat country of western Kansas. Anka worked as a laborer in the construction business, and Florentine worked at cleaning houses to make ends meet. Anka said the family owned three cars, and he hadn't paid a total of a thousand dollars for all three.

At our church supper where they spoke, the family asked to keep their identities a secret because authorities from Romania were still looking for them. But I've never met any family that was any happier! Their gratitude was contagious. They were tickled to be living in the United States!

Compared to the Jucans and Willy Penner, do the rest of us really suffer? Yet their gratitude overflows. In calling at the hospital, I find patients in pain who are able to find many blessings for which they are thankful. Surely a healthy perfectionist can be grateful, too! We can practice gratitude.

Perfectionism is also an agent in causing physical illness. Studies have shown perfectionism to be the culprit for the following afflictions: high blood pressure, heart attacks, strokes, rheumatoid arthritis, atypical facial pain, peptic ulcers, hypertension, and ulcerative colitis.[7]

In addition, tightness in the neck, shoulders, and back have been traced to perfectionism.[8]

Dr. Prem Fry, Professor of Psychology at Trinity Western University in British Columbia, has done research on the effects of perfectionism. In a study of older adults, she found that the life expectancy of perfectionists was reduced by 51 percent as compared to those who were not perfectionists.[9] In a different study she found some good news. Fry found that perfectionists with type 2 diabetes are better at managing the disease than those who are not perfectionists.[10] But for the most part, perfectionism is a detriment to our health.

We have discussed the most prominent symptoms of perfectionism, even though ongoing research will surely discover more. The side effects of perfectionism are listed below. We have covered all of these except the last two; they will be dealt with in future chapters. Now we will look more closely for practical ways to find healing and wholeness and overcome perfectionism. We begin with the struggle to forgive ourselves.

SYMPTOMS OF PERFECTIONISM

1. Goals set too high
2. Low self-esteem
3. Fear of failure
4. Maximize failures; minimize successes
5. Clinging to past mistakes
6. Procrastination
7. Stress (both cause and effect)
8. Depression
9. Agonizing over decision-making
10. Never say "No"
11. The "shoulds"
12. All-or-nothing thinking
13. Self-pity
14. Physical illness
15. Problems with relationships (Chapter 12)
16. Negative view of the present moment (Chapter 15)

CHAPTER ELEVEN

Forgive Yourself!

"God may forgive us, but we do not forgive ourselves."

—P. T. Forsyth

Ben's face still haunts me. I met him when I taught at a private school for the emotionally disturbed.

Ben looked like any ornery boy down the street: short blond hair, a sprinkling of freckles, mischievous blue eyes.

As a childish prank, he struck a match and threw it over the front seat of his parents' car. The match landed in wiring beneath the dashboard and ignited a powerful explosion.

Ben woke up in the hospital to learn that both parents had died in the explosion. His face was covered with third-degree burns. He would never again look in the mirror without seeing the awful reminder—his scarred face—that he had "murdered" his parents. He avoided looking in the mirror because the burden of guilt was too much to bear.

Although most of us haven't experienced Ben's horrid trauma, we too battle with feeling we actually are forgiven. A great deal of our struggle has nothing to do with anything we could have changed. We had no control over our family environment when we were children. Consequently we also wrestle with shame and false guilt.

Add in those things for which we actually need forgiveness, and we can no longer carry all the excess baggage. We look in the mirror and see a scarred face that just doesn't seem good enough to be forgiven. Why, oh why, can't we feel forgiven?

It was my weekend as chaplain on twenty-four-hour call in the hospital emergency unit. During the night, three college-age men were brought to the hospital: all critically injured in separate car accidents, all caused by excessive drinking. Three sets of parents paced the waiting room floor, wondering if their sons would live or die. Because of the critical condition of their sons and with nothing to do but wait, an immediate bond united us. We slowly walked down silent hospital corridors and groped heavenward for answers.

Each parent claimed to feel guilt. In each case I assured them they had done nothing wrong. They could not have changed what happened. They could not have stopped the accidents. Each son was old enough to make his own choice, and it was too late to change that choice.

Each parent was feeling false guilt, but I had to admit that having been in their shoes, my feelings would have been similar. At the same time, our problem with forgiveness could be greatly reduced if we put the shame and false guilt behind us. This process involves two steps: (1) asking ourselves what we could have changed, vowing not to feel guilty for those events we could not change, and (2) finding healing for the inner child. Judging by the number of books about those two subjects, it is no simple, easy task.

Pat answers will not suffice. Talking to a credentialed counselor will help. Individual therapy, group therapy, journaling of dreams, journaling of feelings, and the exploration of those subconscious memories can all be beneficial.

Biblical perfection begins with our genuine confession to God. It sometimes takes a crisis for this to occur. David was a man after God's own heart (I Samuel 13:14). But it was not until Nathan the prophet confronted him with his dual sins of adultery and murder that he was willing to confess them. David's prayer in Psalm 51 reveals the gut-wrenching anguish of his confession.

When sin is mentioned, we usually think, "Oh, they're talking about someone else." We all are prone to ignoring our own sins. We neglect our pride and selfishness. We ignore our competitive strife and jealousy. We forget about starving people throughout the world when we sit down to thank God for our food. John the Elder summed it up well; "If we say we have no sin, we deceive ourselves, and the truth is not in us" (I John 1:8).

One morning I was struggling through the difficult waters of the book of Leviticus. Bored with the laws about leprosy, I asked, "Lord, isn't there anything in this passage that applies to my Christian walk?"

God whispered back, "Leprosy is unclean; sin is unclean. The great care in identifying and purifying leprosy illustrates how much I hate sin."

Reluctantly, I yielded. Leprosy didn't apply to me, but the impurity of sin certainly did. The book of Leviticus challenges us to walk in the holiness of God.

There are only two alternatives mentioned by the writer of First John. If we deny our sin, blocking confession, fellowship with God is cut off. The other alternative is confession and God's forgiveness. By our individual confession God opens the channels to commune and communicate with God. After David confesses his sins of adultery and murder to God, he is overwhelmed by knowing the joy of God's forgiveness (Psalm 32).

The only conditions for receiving God's forgiveness are confession and believing God is able to forgive all sin. If God can forgive David's sins of adultery and murder, God can forgive all sin. Ben with the scarred face is sure he can't be forgiven. Though he feels he has "murdered" his parents, God is able to forgive Ben's sin, too. The Bible assures, "If we confess our sins, God is faithful and just to forgive us our sins and to cleanse us from all unrighteousness" (I John 1:9).

At a retreat, we were asked to list our sins on index cards. Afterward we prayed for God's forgiveness of those sins. Then we placed the index cards in the campfire. As we watched them burn, we understood our sins to be forgiven, destroyed, covered by the blood of Jesus.

What victory and assurance in knowing our sins are covered, blotted out! "Though your sins are like scarlet, they shall be as white as snow" (Isaiah 1:18)! In referring to our forgiveness G. K. Chesterton writes, "God paints in many colors, but He never paints so gorgeously as when He paints in white."[1]

Since believers also sin, forgiveness can never be considered only a one-time act. P. T. Forsyth believes repentance must continue until the time of *telios*, the time of final perfection; he says, "In our perfection there is a permanent element of repentance. The final symphony of praise has a deep bass of penitence."[2] Thankfully, as the Holy Spirit reveals our sin, we learn to confess it right away.

Then the doubts and the questions about whether we are truly forgiven close in on us. Walter Hilton, in *The Stairway of Perfection*, has an answer for those enemies who say we have not been properly absolved of our sins: "...Don't believe this suggestion. It's a lie. You have been properly forgiven in confession."[3] God forgives as we confess.

Hard as it may be for the perfectionist to fathom, forgiveness is possible only because of God's grace. We don't deserve it. It doesn't cost anything because Christ has given His body and blood for the forgiveness of our sins. We cannot earn it. It's free! Every perfectionist could use an extra helping of God's grace! Augustine held a permissive view of grace; he said, "Love God and do as you please." The perfectionist could wipe out several of the symptoms mentioned in the last chapter by following this maxim.

The Scripture is also adamant about the importance of forgiving our neighbor. After the *Paster Noster*, or Lord's Prayer, Jesus said, "For if you forgive others their trespasses, your heavenly Father will also forgive you; but if you do not forgive others, neither will your Father forgive your trespasses" (Matthew 6:14–15). The gospel points out that forgiving others is not just an option; it is a necessity if we are to receive forgiveness ourselves. When evil is done to us, we are always tempted to get even. If we do, we hurt ourselves more than the evildoer. Romans 12 offers clear instruction: "Do not repay anyone evil for evil" (verse 17); "Do not be overcome by evil, but overcome evil with good" (verse 21).

Robyn Halley had just endured the horror of the tragic shooting of her husband by warring gang members. After five hours in surgery, her husband of nearly nineteen years was dead. Yet Robyn could say of the fifteen-year-old gang member who killed him, "I am not bitter toward him."[4] Her son, seventeen-year-old Kenneth, said of his father's death, "I felt like my heart had been ripped out of my chest."[5] But Kenneth could also say, "I'm not bitter toward the person who killed my dad."[6] The news article in *The Wichita Eagle* had stressed the husband's faith, as well as the family's faith. Their vibrant faith and subsequent forgiveness was a great witness of God's love to their community.

Peter assumed he was being extremely lenient when he asked Jesus, "If my brother sins against me, how often should I forgive? As many as seven times?" (Matthew 18:21). After all, Peter had taken the Rabbinic law requiring three times, doubled it, and added one.

Jesus' answer must have been a great surprise. "Not seven times, but, I tell you, seventy times seven." Some translations will say Jesus' instructions were to forgive seventy-seven times. But the point is not how many times, but that we must forgive an unlimited number of times. Just as God forgives us an unlimited number of times, so are we commanded to forgive over and over again. As God persists in forgiving us, we too are challenged to forgive repeatedly.

Jesus continues His answer by telling a parable about the need to forgive our neighbor (Matthew 18:21–35). We'll call the main character by the name of Van Krupped. He is a man deep in debt, so far in debt he owes 20,000 years of wages! Jesus said Van owed 10,000 talents; one talent equals twenty years of wages. He owes millions! He's beyond bankruptcy!

How did Van Krupped acquire such a great debt? Did he order every item in every mail order catalogue? Maybe he frequented Saks Fifth Avenue with a charge card. Did he make poor investments in real estate or oil? Or he might have used a multitude of credit cards and paid the minimum payment every month.

Whatever the cause, Van reaches the last strand of a smoldering rope. The king threatens: pay up or watch your wife and children sold as slaves. Hand over millions or go to jail. Van can hear the sound of steel locks slamming together behind him as he ponders the reality of prison. Wiping his brow, he pleads for mercy. "Be patient with me, and I will pay back everything."

Van perspires, awaiting the verdict. He expects to see prison guards ready to escort him when he hears unbelievable words from the king.

"Forgiven! Cancelled!"

Free, Van leaves before the king has the opportunity to change his mind. He runs across an old friend who owes him a few dollars. He grabs him by the throat and yells, "Pay up or debtors' prison!"

His friend says familiar words: "Be patient with me, and I'll pay you back."

Van refuses to forgive the tiny debt. Word about Van's unwillingness to forgive filters back to the king.

The king is furious and calls for the guards to escort Van before him again. The king thunders, "Why didn't you forgive, just like I forgave you?"

In anger, the king turns Van Krupped over to the jailer until he can pay back the entire debt.

Jesus concludes His story with these words: "This is how your heavenly Father will treat each of you unless you forgive your neighbor from your heart."

Talk about a gargantuan difference in debts! God forgives us many times over what we could possibly forgive our neighbor. What a gigantic debt God cancels! As God freely extends grace to us, likewise we are to offer grace to others.

Only sixteen years of age, Sara Weaver watched a government sniper kill her mother. Sara's brother and U. S. Marshall Degan were also killed in a nine-day standoff at Ruby Ridge, Idaho in August of 1992. Sara's father, Randy Weaver, was being investigated for suspected ties to white supremacist and anti-government groups. Randy Weaver was also accused of selling two illegal sawed-off shotguns to a government informant. Rather than cooperate with the government, he holed up in the family's cabin on a mountain top known as Ruby Ridge. He was arrested, but eventually acquitted of the most serious charges.

Ruby Ridge escalated into a cause for later violence including the Branch Davidian siege in Waco, Texas in 1993 and the Oklahoma City bombing in 1995. Timothy McVeigh claimed both Ruby Ridge and the Branch Davidian violence as the impetus for his bombing of the Alfred P. Murrah building in Oklahoma City.

Sara Weaver talks of how much she misses her mother. "It's hard to live without her to turn to. I want to turn to my mother for advice. We miss her terribly. It never goes away."[7]

Sara battled depression, post-traumatic stress disorder, and "toxic bondage" as well as bitterness and anger at the government.

Twenty years later, she has found forgiveness. She became a born-again Christian. "I went ten years without understanding how to heal. All bitterness and anger had to go. I forgave those who pulled the trigger."[8]

In 2003 Sara met with a childhood friend from Ruby Ridge, and that helped her to make a major turnaround. Her friend spoke of a positive relationship with Jesus Christ.

Sara said, "I decided I was broken and need to be fixed."[9]

Sara Weaver began reading the Bible where she learned that "Jesus commands us to forgive."

She now speaks to Christian groups around the country and has a book published: *From Ruby Ridge to Freedom.*

I remember my grandfather and great-grandfather watching "Amos and Andy" at noon every day. Even though I was pretty young, I still hear them laughing at the two actors. There was a huge man who would always slap Andy across the chest. When Andy had taken it as long as he could, he said to Amos, "I fixed him. I put a stick of dynamite in my pocket. The next time he slaps me his hand will get blown off." In reality, Andy's chest was about to be blown away, too.

Forgiveness is like that. We hurt ourselves much more when we do not forgive than we hurt the other person in need of forgiveness. Jesus reminds us we can lock out God's forgiveness by not forgiving our neighbor. Forgiveness is not ours to hoard. But we fail to forgive because we think it keeps us in control. We seethe and find no desire to let the villain off the hook.

Not long ago, I unwittingly hurt someone's feelings with my insensitive words. Soon after that, she called and told me how much she was hurt. I told her that I didn't intend any harm and that I was sorry. She said it was all right. She accepted my apology. After that, we both dropped it. One apology and one acceptance was enough. For either of us to mention it again would simply open old wounds.

I appreciate her forgiveness. By seeing her example, I plan to offer forgiveness to the next person who needs it. Maturity allows us to forgive and go on with life without continuing to dwell on a misunderstanding or permitting bitterness to drive a wedge between friends.

Who is the most difficult person for a perfectionist to forgive?

Himself! Herself! We hang on to past tests, performances, conversations, and failures. We refuse to let go. We cling to false guilt even when circumstances could not have been changed. In most cases, there will be no second chance, so it won't help to relive it. And I've found that when there is a second chance, it seldom changes the outcome. Most perfectionists I've known have well-developed consciences. That makes it even more difficult to forgive ourselves.

In his book, *Reaching for the Invisible God*, Philip Yancey writes of a man named Bud who works with drug addicts. Bud discovered there is "one key in determining whether individual drug addicts can be cured; if they deeply believe they are a forgivable child of God. Not a failure-free child of God, a forgivable one."[10] The chief goal for us as perfectionists is to understand ourselves as a forgivable child of God. Can we actually believe that we are forgivable?

God always forgives us. When asked, our neighbors usually forgive us. But that accomplishes little if we cannot forgive ourselves. For your own sake, for your own healing, for your assurance and confidence, forgive yourself!

Scott Peck gives another reason it's important to forgive ourselves. In his book, *People of the Lie*, he writes, "Since God forgives us, to fail to forgive ourselves is to hold ourselves higher than God— thereby indulging in the sin of a perverted form of pride."[11]

I was called by the Sheriff's Department to offer counseling to a twenty-three-year-old man who had accidentally run over a bicyclist. Henry had worked the night shift and was driving home from work. He must have momentarily dozed at the steering wheel before hitting the biker and killing her. Henry could still see the pain in the face of her fiancée who was cycling with her. Slumped over a desk, head in arms, tears flowing freely, Henry asked, "What is the worst mistake you ever made?"

Although Henry was sure that was the worst mistake he had ever made, he didn't really need to hear about my worst mistake. What he needed was assurance that this was an accident. In my best tone of consoling, I gave him that assurance. Over a period of months and many hours of counseling, Henry was gradually able to forgive himself and go on with life. Yes, there is still a traumatic memory in Henry's mind, a memory that will never vanish. But the important thing is that he has forgiven himself.

I hope you can forget the scars on your face, Ben. Yes, the trauma of your accident hurts, but if Henry can forgive himself, you can, too. If God can forgive David's sins of adultery and murder, God can forgive all our sins. You can forgive yourself. And we all look better in the mirror when we can forgive ourselves.

CHAPTER TWELVE

Forging Friendships

"A friend is one
To whom we may pour
Out all the contents
Of one's heart,
Chaff and grain together
Knowing that the
Gentlest of hands
Will take and sift it,
Keep what is worth keeping
And with a breath of kindness
Blow the rest away."

—Arabian Proverb

Rachel and Andrea overflow with joy when they are with their friends. It doesn't matter what the activity might be—going to a movie, staying up all night, or playing after school—all activities are more fun with a friend. A recent Friday night set off a mountaintop experience. Each daughter had a friend spend the night. Rachel watched a video with two other friends until 1:30 in the morning. Their joy increased, but mine didn't. At midnight, I took my sleeping bag and pillow to the church. Glenda stayed at home to join the fun.

Deep inside, all of us long for a true friend. The media can't provide this friend. Although we may be influenced by media heroes such as Michael Jordan or the late Mother Teresa or Bill Gates or Oprah Winfrey, none of these can be a true friend. They aren't available when we really need them. Perfectionists also long for a true friend, but have difficulty with long-term relationships.

At a very early age, children discover the difficulty of forging friendships. I use the word, "forge," to mean something specific here: that is, the dictionary definition, "to form through heating and hammering." All relationships require some heating and hammering, some necessary conflict, some give and take. The perfectionist, however, finds more difficulties than others in forging friendships.

The perfectionist prefers to forget rather than form friendships. According to Marian Woodman, the perfectionist prefers being task-oriented above being person-oriented. She writes, "To strive for perfection is to kill love because perfection does not recognize humanity."[1] Accomplishing the perfect job usually rates higher than forging a perfect relationship to a perfectionist.

For that reason, I've found some advantages in being married to a perfectionist. Glenda won't let me take the Christmas decorations down. She's afraid I'll break them. Granted, all her collector's ornaments spread out on the tree make quite a beautiful sight! But she also objects to all the time it takes her to take every one of them down. The subtle hint? "I need some help."

Sorry, it's either choice A or choice B. But I'm glad she has such high standards in protecting those Christmas decorations!

Paul Rom states that perfectionists end up nervous, self-conscious, and self-critical; they discourage others and alienate others from themselves.[2] They become isolated human beings, longing to relate in a friendly manner but unable to develop long-lasting relationships.[3] Indeed, the counselors I know would agree with David Stoop's statement: "Most relationship problems I encounter in my counseling stem from some form of perfectionism."[4]

Perfectionists expect from others the same high standards they impose upon themselves. Perfection is expected of parents, teachers, siblings, and friends. Reforming those they live with becomes a pet project; they strive to perfect the imperfect residents in their home.

Miriam Adderholdt-Elliot states, "They have a bad habit of criticizing anyone who doesn't live up to their expectations or dares to make mistakes."[5] That criticism drives people away.

I confess to falling for this trap without even realizing it. As a former basketball referee, I was taught that the cardinal sin is to raise the arms when observing a foul and go through the hand signals without ever blowing the whistle. I watched that happen twice at a recent game and found myself yelling vehemently at the referee. I later apologized to her and explained why I got so upset. She accepted my apology. But I realized that unconsciously, I had expected her standards to be the same as mine. She had less experience, and I didn't allow her to make a mistake, to be human.

Perfectionists are also slow to open up to others. Those who live with a perfectionist will find it difficult to get to know the real person. "Perfectionists will work just as hard at keeping others from knowing them as they will at changing others,"[6] states Stoop.

Further alienation of others stems from an attitude of superiority toward them. Those around perfectionists are frequently made to feel inferior. "Playing 'look what you've done to me' enters into most of their relationships,"[7] writes James Jolliff. They leave emotionally wounded victims behind. The result of all this harsh treatment of others is depression and loneliness for the perfectionist. While all relationships endure periods of withdrawal and closeness, the perfectionist is usually in the withdrawal stage.

Our relationships—starting with our openness to become intimate with others—are entirely dependent upon our self-esteem. Self-esteem is defined as how we see ourselves, how we picture our worth and competence. Our self-esteem is based on the affirmation and support we received from our parents when we were children. Surprisingly, children with the same parents, environment, and experiences can show contrasting levels of self-esteem.

Some basic fundamentals will develop self-esteem. Feeling a sense of unconditional love is the most important. Parents add to self-esteem when they assure the child it's all right to fail as long as something positive is learned from the experience. Self-esteem grows when we are sure that we have given the best effort possible.

Attainable goals are a necessity because the perfectionist usually sets goals too high, doesn't make them, and loses self-esteem.

A few small steps over a long period of time plus a disciplined commitment to carry them out build self-esteem. The first step to self-esteem is to stop blaming a parent, spouse, ex-spouse, etc. and take responsibility for your own individual decisions. Current problems are not caused entirely by what one or two members of the family have done to us. According to Harriet Lerner in *The Dance of Intimacy*, often they go back to a multi-generational network of patterns.[8] In other words, we depend upon preceding generations for our present behavior including strengths and failures.

Striving to connect with our nuclear family builds self-esteem. We may resist taking such a huge risk, but it is necessary for our own healing. If the risk is never conquered, how can our confidence grow?

One way to build self-esteem is to exercise. Vigorous exercise makes us more confident. A friend of mine swears that since he began running regularly twenty years ago, confidence has spilled over in all other avenues he pursues.

Anything a parent or teacher can do to heighten self-esteem in children is a worthwhile investment in the future. Andrea's first grade teacher, Mrs. Coles, sets aside an entire week for each student to be "special." The student has designated jobs to perform. The bulletin board displays pictures of the child's family and child's favorites. Mrs. Coles makes a laminated book as a keepsake. What a constructive way to establish self-esteem for the child!

Once self-esteem goes up, the perfectionist turns out more vulnerable and more open with others. Intimate relationships require honesty and transparency with others. Augustus Napier and Carl Whitaker stress the importance of the ability to be separate: "People can't risk being close unless they have the ability to be separate—it's too frightening to be deeply involved if you aren't sure you can be separate and stand on your own."[9] Intimacy demands interdependence: a confidence to be able to stand alone, as well as sensitivity to the other's needs. To be able to stand alone—separate from a loved one—also requires trust.

It is important to recognize some limits in our relationships. There are qualitative limits; how much can I offer to one relationship? There are quantitative limits; with how many people can I have a close relationship at once? Though Jesus could have traveled with many more disciples or followers, it is no coincidence that the number was twelve. Since Jesus was fully human, how many people could He relate well to at one time?

Henri Nouwen in his book, *The Wounded Healer*, decries the tragedy of a suffering man or woman who goes to a minister and finds only "aloofness."[10] He states, "The paradox indeed is that those who want to be for 'everyone' find themselves often unable to be close to anyone."[11] You see, anyone who takes serving others seriously, anyone who works in a service-oriented job, is advised not to extend care toward too many persons. For a lack of compassion will result.

On the other hand, it is crucial to increasing connectedness with others that the relationships with the "family of origin" become close. If there is no receptivity from those in the immediate family, if all efforts to connect with immediate family feel like we navigate a one-way street, then our journey results in a dead-end. But we must still persist in trying to connect with parents and siblings. It may take time, but we must give ourselves every opportunity to re-connect. These relationships with parents and siblings are the foundation for all other relationships.

In his book, *Pastor and Parish,* Dr. E. M Pattison has visualized a wonderful system necessary for healthy relationships.[12] He says it takes four groups to hold up the trampoline upon which each of us bounces: immediate or nuclear family, extended family (aunts, uncles, cousins, grandparents, etc.), life-long friends, and associates (defined as acquaintances from work, church, or recreation). Often through the grace of God, when one side has not been held up, when one group was lacking, God has miraculously designated a "surrogate" to provide for that need.

King David must have felt the same when he wrote, "Though my father and mother forsake me, the LORD will receive me" (Psalm 27:10).

Not long ago, I did some inspirational reading about what a true friend is. I began reminiscing about friends, from the distant past through the present. An uplifting, strengthening experience flooded over me as I remembered first one friend, then another. I made a list of all those friends who had offered a positive influence on me throughout my life.

A number of true friends come quickly to mind. David Cox, six days older than me, who drowned in a farm pond when we were sixteen. Merle and Ruth Roe, grandparents who were never late with a birthday present. Dave Baker and Ollie Dongell, seminary friends who offered a lively joke and constant support. Don Joy, seminary professor who related with our small group once a week, one unafraid to "speak the truth in love." Tiny Sweetland, the Christian layman who went calling with me every Monday night when we easily could have been distracted by Monday Night Football. And Glenda, my wife, who spent her last dime on steak when we dated. I promptly burned those steaks on the grill!

I remember Edith Glover, a loving children's church leader; Lloyde Johnson, my high school Sunday School teacher and Christian bookstore owner; and Bill and Lois Wells, high school youth sponsors. Kip Ryherd, always ready for a golf game. My Dad always took us to the gym to play basketball on Sunday afternoons. My Mom cooked the most scrumptious meals. My brothers always joked around. Their humor always cheers me up!

Our daughters, Rachel and Andrea, hold the trampoline up with their uplifting encouragement. Rachel has always been my best cheerleader for marathons and the long bike rides. Andrea lights up our lives with her humor. I see lots of aunts and uncles and forty-one first cousins holding my trampoline up. There are more I could name around the trampoline, but to imagine this group holding me up gives me an overwhelming sense of confidence.

I can form a definition of friendship from remembering the ways these people around the trampoline have been a friend to me. The following concept of friendship doesn't come from any book, but from seeing it lived out in the ways each one has been a genuine friend to me.

What is a friend? A friend is someone unafraid to put us on a pedestal in the sense of respecting us, someone who has high ideals for us, someone who thinks the best of us. A friend is someone who restores trust in us when others have betrayed it. Someone not demanding in ways that hurt, but still able to motivate us by example. Someone who is available when we most need help.

A friend is someone who is committed to decisions that are best for the long haul. Someone unafraid to carry out the most menial of tasks. Someone who, down to the last dime, still fixes a meal with a willingness to share. Someone unafraid to share the truth, even when it hurts. Friendship does not have to be earned, but is given unconditionally. These qualities are those we would want in a friend, and they are likewise characteristics we can give to others as a friend.

I would encourage you to spend some time remembering your friends, too. There have surely been some times, possibly after a move, when it felt like there were only a few friends to hold up that side of the trampoline. But there were other times, perhaps in college, when that side of the trampoline was mighty full. Reflection on this group of friends has brought an immense sense of gratitude that God brought all of them my way. We can all be buoyed by friends who hold up the trampoline.

"There is a friend that sticks closer than a brother" is how the Bible puts it (Proverbs 18:24). Jesus of Nazareth met all these standards of friendship. Restoring trust. Fixing breakfast. Washing feet. Offering his body. Loving unconditionally. And then he dared to call his disciples friends (John 15:15, NRSV). Notice the reason Jesus gives for calling them friends: "…because I have made known to you everything that I have heard from my Father." Jesus even shared the good news and teaching that came directly from His Father.

Intimate relationships have never originated in the hearts of humans, but in the compassionate loving heart of God. "Love is from God; everyone who loves is born of God and knows God" (I John 4:7b,c). Therefore, close relationships to others depend upon a close relationship with God.

In speaking of how perfection is defined in terms of the Old Testament covenant, Hans La Rondelle says, "Personal perfection is not described in terms of a sinless nature, but of gracious fellowship with the holy and merciful covenant God."[13] The vacuum of loneliness felt by all people cannot be filled completely by the companionship of another human, but begins with the Divine invitation to commune with God. The road to perfection begins with our acceptance of that invitation.

Forge some friendships. We all look better in the mirror when there are friends in the picture.

CHAPTER THIRTEEN

Embracing God

"The suppression of the spiritual is the real
pathology of our times."

—Viktor Frankl

I remember a conversation with Rachel when she was five—a talk I would like to forget. She had been perceptive in observing my duties as pastor; she had also picked up opinions of those in the congregation. I made a mistake and apologized to her. "It's OK, Dad." she said. "You're not perfect." End of conversation—I thought.

She paused for effect, and then added, "Even if some people think you are." The pastor might have fooled some in the congregation, but not this young realist! Dad was only human to his daughter.

One parishioner thought I was perfect; that meant I was able to predict the weather. A church we served had a standing reservation for the second Sunday evening of the month when they would have a supper, business meeting, and program. One month, the only time our family could go on vacation was the second Sunday. The church members understood, and we moved the monthly supper to the third Sunday.

The only problem was a blizzard that bombarded us on the third Sunday. A lady from the church called to tell us the supper was cancelled. Then she said, "Of course, if we had met on the usual night, we wouldn't have to worry about it."

I'm sorry; I should have known a snowstorm would hit ahead of time. Being perfect can take its toll! I'd rather be human.

We expect so much in a world spoiled by instant gratification and advanced technology. To our success-driven society, "fail" and "lose" are the worst of four-letter words. The current generation is the best generation at spotting fallacies; faults receive more attention than traits of integrity. James Jolliff gives the example of the man whose wife had a gap between her teeth.[1] He constantly compared her mouth to the mouths of other women. He actually planned on leaving her because of the gap between her teeth.

Though this sounds extreme, numerous examples of such picky people in our culture surround us. Consider the parent who constantly nags when the gifted child makes a mistake. Or the parent who does the child's homework rather than trusting the child to do it.

We won't have to look far to find some real nitpickers. There are people who will have nothing to do with a business company because of the color of their carpet. Think of children who complain about being served the wrong kind of cookies. There are people who won't listen to an elderly person if the clothes don't match. A teacher recommends to her church that they buy one color for children's bags because otherwise the children will fight over who takes which color. Being picky keeps perfectionists from enjoying life. As Will Rogers once said, "It's great to be great, but it's greater to be human."[2]

Unrealistic expectations of the perfectionist cause much suffering. Henri Nouwen says, "Many people have suffered because of the false supposition on which they have based their lives. That supposition is that there should be no fear or loneliness, no confusion or doubt."[3] Indeed, fear and anxiety are two of the basic causes for perfectionism. There can be no perfect world; there always will be pain and loneliness. There can be no perfect self; there always will be fear and anxiety.

Really now, would a perfect world be any fun at all? Imagine a world that offers no room for growth. A world where there are no goals toward which to strive. The perfectionist wouldn't be happy in that world either.

We learn from our mistakes. We learn to walk from our tumbles as a toddler. As our first-grader learns to read, the words she struggles with most are the ones she'll remember next time. The words missed on a spelling test will be spelled correctly the next time. It is mistakes, painful as they may be, teaching us valuable lessons and motivating us to overcome the next time. Our greatest learning experiences stem from our worst mistakes and our worst failures. Failure only seems devastating; actually, it's the onset of learning.

Therefore, parents and teachers must allow children to make minor mistakes. Of course, we want to protect them from mistakes that can be critical, like failing to look both ways before crossing the highway. But if the child isn't allowed to make mistakes, learning experiences are eliminated. If trivial mistakes are inexcusable in the home, the child is afraid of trying at all. The fear of failure keeps the child from trying and learning subsequent lessons.

It's the same with the spiritual walk. We must come to a sense of our own failings, our own inadequacies, our own sins before we will seek God. Only when we reach the end or our rope do we ask for God's help. Hans La Rondelle states, "We are struck by the fact that man in every culture never has been satisfied with himself as he was. He was always on his way, striving for, searching for a perfection which he believed would restore him to the original perfection he must have had…"[4]

Scads of people feel a need to find perfection before approaching God. No concept could be further from the truth. This is like assuming we must master every bit of information in the Library of Congress before starting kindergarten. Even if we happened to be perfect, it wouldn't make us more worthy of approaching God. God wants us to approach Him in spite of our unworthiness. From the standpoint of our awareness, the road toward God begins with confession. God wants to approach us. The Hound of Heaven was seeking each of us before we were born.

The quandary—like admitting our mistakes—is coming to God to confess our sin. The most difficult step is admitting our need. Thomas à Kempis points toward our double standard when he says, "We would willingly have others perfect, and yet we amend not our own faults."[5] It's as if we cannot see ourselves in the mirror, but cannot miss the faults of others. How blind we are to our own faults when we look in the mirror! The perfectionist longs to see a perfect image in the mirror, so we deny our sin.

Thomas Wilson, also aware of our blindness, contends, "The greatest of all disorders is to think we are whole, and need no help."[6] George Fox directs us out of the quagmire with these words, "The light which shows us our sins is the light which heals us."[7] The psalmist says, "It is good for me that I was humbled, so that I might learn your statutes" (Psalm 119:176). In reality, we are far from perfect, and we dare not fake it, or we won't grow at all.

The road to perfection begins not with our own efforts, but as the grace of God works within us. Therefore, we discover perfection much different than perfectionism. We take the first step with a God who is perfect; that first step doesn't begin with our feeble efforts.

There are a multitude of references to "perfection" in the Bible and the devotional classics. The Bible uses "perfect" 108 times in various grammatical forms. The problem, however, is that there are several ways to interpret "perfection" in the Bible. Our task is to look at a sampling of these interpretations and develop our own scriptural understanding of perfection. While taking markedly different views on Christian perfection, the devotional classics can also gently guide us toward an understanding of perfection that will offer healing. The simple beauty of these writings inspires us in our call to perfection.

During the late 1800's, Andrew Murray wrote of a universal need in humanity to desire perfection; "God hath wrought into every human heart a deep desire after perfection."[8] Murray says the longing for perfection is unanimous. Evelyn Underhill says, "Here we are, small half-real creatures of sense and spirit, haunted by the sense of a Perfection ever calling to us, and yet ourselves so fundamentally imperfect, so hopelessly involved in an imperfect world…"[9] John Wesley in *A Plain Account of Christian Perfection* proclaims, "For what is the most perfect creature in heaven or earth in Thy presence, but a void capable of being filled with Thee and by Thee…"[10] It is unfortunate that today, even among believers, we find little awareness of a calling to perfection.

Jean-Pierre de Caussade (1675—1751) said his vows as a priest in Toulouse, France. He taught Greek, Latin, and philosophy. In 1729 de Caussade was appointed spiritual director for visitation nuns; he alternated between serving at Nancy and Toulouse. He preached throughout southern and central France. In 1740 he became rector of a Jesuit college in Perpignan. He risked punishment from the church because he taught that perfection was available to everyone, opposing the official stance of the Catholic Church who taught perfection accessible only to contemplatives. Countering the official Church is most likely why he went through so many changes in position and location.

De Caussade asserts, "I wish to make all see that everyone can aspire, not to the same specific things, but to the same love, the same surrender, the same God and his work, and thereby achieve the most perfect saintliness."[11] We can aspire to the same love, but perfect saintliness seems like a stretch for many on this side of heaven. De Caussade also thought our efforts in searching for a theology of perfection rather useless—considering God had already provided the means to perfection. He claims, "I suggest we are like sick doctors trying to cure patients in perfect health."[2]

God's grace abounds! That exclamation gives hope for the perfectionist. Andrew Murray says, "… The Christian can receive the witness of the Spirit that the Father sees and accepts in him the perfect heart, even when there is not yet the perfect performance."[13] God does not expect a perfect performance, just a perfect heart. One alarming Scripture to the perfectionist is Matthew 5:48; Jesus commands us to "be perfect, as your Father in heaven is perfect." The good news is that Jesus is not talking about the performance, but the love in our hearts. The context of this passage tells us to love our enemies, so that the only expectation for perfection commands us to love.

P. T. Forsyth perceives the working of God's grace in a similar manner. "Beethoven was not troubled when a performer struck a wrong note, but he was angry when he failed with the spirit and idea of the piece. So with the Great Judge and Artist of Life."[14] And to fail with the spirit of the piece, we would have to be in all-out rebellion against God.

We can be guided gradually toward perfection by a God who is Perfect. Again, Matthew 5:48 refers to "...your Father in heaven (Who) is perfect." In the Old Testament Yahweh is repeatedly pictured as Perfect. "The Rock, His work is perfect" (Hebrew=*tamim*); (Deuteronomy 32:4). "As for God His way is perfect--*tamim*" (II Samuel 22:31). "As for God, His way is perfect--*tamim*. The LORD's way is flawless; He shields all who take refuge in Him" (Psalm 18:30). "The law of the LORD is perfect (*temimah*), reviving the soul; the testimony of the LORD is sure, making wise the simple" (Psalm 19:7). La Rondelle says, "His 'perfection' is only described in terms of relationships with man and with His covenant people in particular."[15]

The perfectionist can never know wholeness by trying to work for it. How, then, can anyone find wholeness? The Bible mentions the possibility of perfection for humans only in covenant relationship with a Perfect God. Healing for perfectionism springs from this covenant relationship. Wholeness for perfectionists flows from this covenant relationship. A new God-given confidence wells up within us. We are now free to fail, assured that God's love for us doesn't waver with our performance. In contrast, our culture looks for results first with little concern for how they are achieved.

Perfection will not come immediately, but only by a lengthy process of growth. Murray contends, "This is not the work of a day... . . . There is nothing at times that appears more mysterious to the believer than the slowness of God."[16] De Caussade describes this unfolding as a beautiful tapestry.[17] We see only the side being sewn, the side with little design, without seeing the beauty of the work until it is completed. While it is being woven, we behold no sign of its artistry.

Other theologians agree. Gregory of Nyssa envisioned a "gradual advance of the earnest Christian toward perfection."[18] Laurence Wood believes perfection to be consistent with the doctrine of dispensations,[19] including a divine interpretation of history and the different ages of that history. Ives Congar finds perfection compatible with the Roman Catholic view of various stages of the Christian life.[20]

This perfection is attained exclusively through the means of God's grace. An unknown author in *The Cloud of Knowing* asserts, "To this perfection, and all other, our Lord Jesus Christ calls us to Himself in the gospel: where He bids *that we should be perfect* by grace *as He Himself* is by nature."[21]

This grace leads us to be transformed into a reflection of Jesus Christ. It points toward the Biblical mirror found in II Corinthians 3:18: "And all of us, with unveiled faces, seeing the glory of the Lord as though reflected in a mirror, are being transformed into the same image from one degree of glory to another..." The mirror from which we gain real fulfillment is the one reflecting the image of Christ. We are being transformed into His likeness.

In a fitting illustration, C. S. Lewis shows how perfection comes about by the grace of God working in our lives.[22] Lewis compared it to having a toothache during his childhood. The tooth hurt very much, but he would not say anything to his mother. He knew what dentists were like; if he went in for a single toothache, the dentist would find many more teeth in need of repair. Of dentists Lewis knew that "if you gave them an inch, they would take an ell."[23] The word, ell, has become obsolete, but meant forty-five inches in England during Lewis's day. God's grace is quietly working to perfect us, even in those areas where we consciously are not aware of the need to be perfected.

The basketball coach for my seminary team spent hours and hours fine tuning the skill of boxing out. It is a technique to keep an offensive player from getting inside position for a rebound. Moving laterally helps to keep the offensive player from getting inside. A skilled player uses his hands to feel where the offensive player is going. To box out also requires using the legs, hips, and elbows to keep the player outside.

When our daughters were playing basketball in junior high and senior high, people in the crowd learned to stay away from sitting next to me. I would be helping our daughters along by physically boxing out in the stands. My fear is that we've boxed out God. We didn't mean to eliminate God from the schedule, but other activities block out our time with God.

Psalm 23 paints a similar picture. Two verses tell us the Shepherd leads. "He leads me beside the still waters" (verse 2b); "He leads me in paths of righteousness for His name's sake" (verse 3b). Why does the Shepherd lead? Because the sheep isn't smart enough to know where to go or how to get there. The sheep keeps wandering off because the next tuft of grass looks more appetizing. The sheep didn't intend to leave the Shepherd, but suddenly fears he is lost. The greener grass on the distant hill looks better than the one close by.

Our calendar and daily schedule fills up so fast. We weren't necessarily looking to book all our time with all these activities. There is no time left simply to meet God and listen to God because we've wandered away in search of greener grass.

Our society has developed a severe case of attention deficit disorder. A myriad of today's inhabitants on planet earth cannot go fifteen minutes without texting, talking on a cell phone, or checking e-mail, face book, twitter, a laptop, or a tablet. How can God get our attention if we've boxed God out with our technology? We need to set aside time to meditate on God's word and to listen to God's leading.

Thomas Kelly says, "We Western peoples are apt to think our great problems are external, environmental. We are not skilled in the inner life, where the real roots of our problem lie."[24]

Include God in the plans. Embrace God. Listen to His Word. We'll all look better and feel better by being a reflection of God.

CHAPTER FOURTEEN

Enjoy This Moment

"We must confine ourselves to the present moment without taking thought for the one before or the one to come."
—Jean-Pierre de Caussade

When I was a freshman in high school, we moved to a house five miles from where my grandparents lived. They had been wanting to plant a huge garden for years, but looked out their back window to see a tiny back yard not much bigger than a postage stamp. We now looked out our back yard to see acres of fertile land. My grandparents decided to plant a big garden behind our house.

Much to my surprise, I was handed a hoe with no explanation of how to use it. It didn't require much technique, just some perspiration. The sun got hotter, and the rows kept getting longer. My hands hurt, and blisters swelled. I kept checking my watch. I looked forward with eager anticipation to the very minute that job would be finished. I was not enjoying the moment.

My mother was pregnant and canned many quarts of green beans that summer. I still picture her massive, swollen feet on our linoleum floor. She's barefoot because no shoes come close to fitting. She had to be looking forward to my brother's birth. She couldn't have been enjoying the present moment either.

The perfectionist is seldom happy with the present moment. Too much time is spent despising the past, leading to depression. We constantly want to re-form the past. Why didn't we act differently? Why couldn't we change the outcome of history? But the past can't be changed.

Or we spend too much time worrying about the future, leading to anxiety. When we are too busy—scurrying from appointment to appointment—we waste time anticipating how to get through the next moment rather than enjoying the present moment. We speculate about what the future holds. We try to change the future before it arrives. We worry about balancing the check book or how the bills will be paid. We need to learn to put the past behind and to trust God with the future.

Living in the past or in the future wipes out our efficiency in the present. It's very to hard to listen to others when we are reliving the past or worrying about the future. Listening skills decline when we're not committed to the present moment. The perfectionist is typically worried about doing many tasks well while losing out on the joy of the present moment.

God spoke some special words to Moses at the burning bush; God said, "I Am Who I Am" (Exodus 3:14). God did not say, "I Was Who I Was." Nor "I Will Be Whom I Will Be." Granted, God was the God of history, the God of the past. True, God will be the God of the future, the Alpha and the Omega, the beginning and the end. But God wanted Moses to recognize the God of the present. Our God is sufficient for this moment.

Because of his disagreement with the Catholic Church, Jean de Caussade was not allowed to publish his work during his lifetime. He was being punished by the Church because he taught that perfection was available to all, not just to contemplatives. De Caussades's desire was that we walk with God in the present moment. We are called to carry out God's purpose for us in the here and now. De Caussade writes, "All we need to know is how to recognize His will in the present moment."[1] Our task is to find God's will in the present and to follow it.

This road leads toward perfection. As Kitty Muggeridge, who translated the latest version of de Caussade's *The Sacrament of the Present Moment,* states in the Preface, "This is the way we can all strive for spiritual perfection in so far as it is available in this life. Pious saint and humble sinner alike will be given the grace to enable them to do so if they truly long for it."[2]

De Caussade's wish was also that we find joy in the present moment. He says, "…With [the virtue of the divine will], [all creation] is brought into the realm of his kingdom where *every moment is complete contentment in God alone*, and a total surrender of all creatures to his order. It is the sacrament of the present moment."[3]

De Caussade goes on to describe the ecstasy, the rapture of perfect love available to all who surrender to doing God's will. Andrew Murray also understands this: "We meet every providential appointment, in every ordinary duty of daily life, as God's will."[4] When divine interruptions appear without warning during our busy day, we can trust God. What seems like a delay to us happens to be God telling us when and where we need to be, so that He can work through us. God plans a better schedule than we do.

This contentment is found in a sense of partnership with God. German scholars termed it *heilsgeschicte*, literally, "salvation-history." It began with God leading the Hebrews out of Egypt, through the wilderness, and into the promised land. It gives us a sense that God is walking with us, guiding each step. Again, de Caussade points to the God behind history, "We must therefore allow each moment to be the cause of the next; the reason for what precedes being revealed in what follows, so that everything is linked firmly and solidly together in a divine chain of events."[5]

In the role of parenting, we also learn to enjoy the moment. The temptation of any parent is to wish the current stage was over. We think "If only our child can get through the terrible two's, everything will be all right." Or, "If I can live through her teenage years without killing someone, I will survive." We might wish for a long-past stage: when the child was just an infant, and we held her close for hours on end. In reality, there is something good about every stage our children go through, and we must focus on the current positives to help them arrive healthy at the next stage.

When Rachel was just a toddler, my Mom offered some meaningful advice. She said, "Savor your time with your children when they are small." Rarely has she offered advice, so it meant more to Glenda and me when she did. We have tried to follow those words of wisdom. I must confess, however, there were times when the girls were little that I counted the minutes until Glenda got home from work or until a church committee meeting. It wasn't that I was dying to arrive at the meeting, but their energy level seemed like more than I could handle. But to paraphrase the above advice: enjoy the present moment with your child.

Perfectionists easily fall prey to a spiraling web of negative thoughts and words. It becomes habit to dwell on what is wrong with the world, rather than what is good about it. James Jolliff says, "I have patients who could find fault with a sunset."[6] It affects everyone around the perfectionist. Frances Touchet has suggested that a high percentage cannot stand the world around them.[7] Something must be done to end this downward spiral.

Biblical guidelines do not condone this negative outlook. Paul instructs the saints at Philippi to think about the following things: "whatever is true, whatever is honorable, whatever is just, whatever is pure, whatever is pleasing, whatever is commendable, if there is any excellence, if there is anything worthy of praise" (Philippians 4:8). Soon after that, Paul says, "For I have learned to be content with whatever I have" (4:11). To the Thessalonian church he also says, "Rejoice always, pray without ceasing, give thanks in all circumstances; for this is the will of God in Christ Jesus for you" (I Thessalonians 5:16–-18). Indeed, we are instructed to be positive in our outlook.

We can't continue to look at everything with the attitude: "What's wrong with this?" The more we see the negative, the sooner we eliminate the positive from life. The more we discover only mistakes, flaws, imperfections, and sins, the harder it becomes to climb out of the pit.

Today I talked with Joy, whose husband of forty-four years was buried a week ago. He had suffered from cancer for a year and a half. Joy said to me, "Everyone says I will get angry, but I never have been angry. And my husband wasn't either. We had a lot of things to be thankful for. I have never been angry about it, and I'm not sure I ever will be." Joy finds strength in focusing on the positive, even in the worst of circumstances. I tried to assure her that it's all right if she ever finds a need to vent strong feelings of grief.

Perfectionists can gradually learn to see the positive. We can create new ways to offer our praise to other persons and ourselves, too. Over time we grow in our affirmation of persons, and we are able to grasp the art of celebrating the achievements of others and ourselves. We discover a lesson in how to affirm the talents and abilities of ourselves and others, too.

Patterns of negative thinking can be changed. An appropriate prescription for perfectionists is recommended by Charles Allen in *God's Psychiatry.* .[8] He instructs the patient to read Psalm 23 five times a day for one week. To be cured, the patient must read the twenty-third Psalm slowly and thoroughly at the following times: when first waking up, after breakfast, lunch, and dinner, and before going to sleep. Like any prescription, the times for medication must be strictly followed. This Psalm changes the perfectionist's pattern of thinking. Continued reading in other Psalms will transform the mind and soul in a constructive way.

One winter I went out to jog. I had been consistent in running four or five days a week. But I'd run very little for three weeks, because of job demands and a debilitating virus. I set a pre-run goal of five miles. After a few strides, my goal quickly dropped to four miles. By two and a half miles, I was alternating between a jog and a walk. I ended up running a little over three miles. Years before, I would have mentally kicked myself for the two miles I didn't run. On this day, I celebrated the three miles I did run.

As perfectionists, it's to our benefit if we can learn to be thankful, even to go as far as to count our blessings. William Ward offers this healing thought in *The Divine Physician*, "Physicians tell us thanksgiving has real therapeutic value. It concentrates our attention on the things we have, instead of letting us complain and fret for the things we think we lack. A psychologist friend mentioned the number of people in a certain mental hospital and added, 'Half are there because they never learned the art of being thankful.'"[8]

Over two centuries ago, William Law wrote, "If any one would tell you the shortest, surest way to all happiness, and all perfection, he must tell you to make a rule to yourself, to thank and praise God for everything that happens to you."[9] Counting our blessings offers powers of healing for the perfectionist. The following verse helps us accent the positive. It's entitled, "Little Things."

> Most of us
> Miss out
> On life's
> Big prizes.
> The Pulitzer.
> The Nobel.
> Oscars.
> Tonys.
> Emmys.
> But we're
> All eligible
> For life's
> Small pleasures.
> A pat
> On the back.
> A kiss
> Behind the ear.
> A four-pound bass.
> A full moon.
> An empty
> Parking space.
> A crackling fire.
> A great meal.
> A glorious sunset.
> Hot soup.

Cold drinks.
Don't fret
About
Copping life's
Grand awards.
Enjoy its
Tiny delights.
There are plenty
For all of us.

Some writers imply that perfectionists are no fun. Marian Woodman says, "One thing that complex hates is fun; it reduces everything to grim responsibility."[11] Miriam Adderholdt-Elliot advises, "Hang around with funny people (Chances are, they won't be perfectionists—an excellent reason all by itself for seeking them out)."[12]

Actually, some perfectionists do have a sense of humor. Andrew Carnegie was once showing a large delegation through his plant when he stopped to talk to a stooped, gray-haired employee.

"Let's see, Wilson," he said. "How many years exactly is it that you've been working for me?"

"Thirty-nine, sir," replied Wilson. "And may I add that in that entire time, I made only one trifling mistake."

"Good work," said Carnegie, "but from now on, please try to be a bit more careful."[13]

Carnegie meant this to be funny. But how many of us—either consciously or unconsciously—expect to have a perfect record?

We can be pretty serious until a crisis hits. Then we use humor to cope with the tough times. Humor is the great compensator for personal and family crisis.

The power of healing in humor has been well-documented by Norman Cousins. He suffered from a serious illness affecting the connective tissue and spent many hours watching the funniest programs he could find on television. He was sure it was the laughter and the humor that brought about his healing. Cousins says, "I made the joyous discovery that ten minutes of genuine belly laughter had an anesthetic effect and would give me at least two hours of pain-free sleep."[14]

Humor can also relax the perfectionist in the classroom. One of Rachel's teachers constantly teased her and her classmates. It made her relax. Her scores weren't nearly as high in other classes because she put more pressure on herself when other teachers were serious. This funny teacher helped her relax with his humor.

Elton Trueblood points out the humor as well as the humanity of Christ in his book, *The Humor of Christ.* He challenges the common picture of Jesus as somber and gloomy. To the contrary, many of Christ's teachings cannot be interpreted without admitting His humorous intent. Trueblood asserts, "Anyone who reads the Synoptic Gospels with a relative freedom from presuppositions might be expected to see that Christ laughed, and that He expected others to laugh…"[15]

As a part of the Apostles' Creed, we profess to "believe in Jesus Christ, who was conceived by the Holy Spirit, born of the Virgin Mary…." This affirmation is based on the theologians' conclusion that Jesus was "fully human and fully divine." Perfectionists find a great deal more difficulty in seeing the human side of Christ.

Why did Jesus want his cousin, John, to baptize Him? It wasn't because He needed forgiveness for His sins. Jesus didn't want baptism as a symbol of purification because He had no need for that. Jesus asked for baptism because He wanted to identify His human side with our human side.

As long as Christ is seen as divine, we do not naturally identify with Him. But imagine His human side. He not only joked, but became tired and hungry, perspired, and felt rejection from earthly parents and siblings. He went through all the trials we do, except for knowing He sinned or made a mistake. Striving to identify with the human side of Jesus Christ would benefit perfectionists.

We perfectionists take ourselves entirely too seriously. Not only do we need to loosen up and lighten up; think of the warmth we can offer to others with our sense of humor. Unfortunately, much of the humor we hear is negative and destructive. We could work at not being so critical and sarcastic toward others with our sense of humor. We perfectionists can learn to use our sense of humor to build self-esteem in other persons. We can be the "salt of the earth" with constructive humor.

We might learn to laugh at ourselves as heartily as we laugh at others. After all, this is a giant step when it comes to enjoying a sense of humor. When we perfectionists can laugh at ourselves, we can laugh at most anything.

We cannot live in the past or in the future. The only moment we can enjoy is the one in the present.

CHAPTER FIFTEEN

A Leisurely Pace

"The action of those whose lives are given to the Spirit has in it something of the leisure of Eternity; and because of this, they achieve far more than those whose lives are enslaved by the rush and hurry, the unceasing tick-tock of the world."

—Evelyn Underhill

The new academic dean of the seminary I attended upset many of the best students. Previously, they had been allowed to take more than a full load of classes. No more. This dean strictly enforced a new rule. No more than fifteen hours per semester. Period. No exceptions. Student after student unloaded complaints about the unfairness of it all.

Then the dean gave the reason for the sudden change in rules. The dean *himself* zipped through what should have been four years of college in two and one half; three years of seminary had taken him only two. Those years were now only a blur in his memory. He didn't want these students to make the same mistake.

I learned a similar lesson from the first 10k race I ran. I wanted to keep up with Sam, my roommate and also a college track coach.

I just thought I knew something about running! My training technique was to increase my mileage every day for a month until I ran seven miles the day before the race. I bought some name-brand running shoes. They had tough, neoprene soles that gave no support or cushion for my feet. I used the worst of training techniques and bought shoes that looked flashy, but destroyed feet and knees.

Well, the gun went off, and so did Sam and his college runners. Like greyhounds, they sped on, encouraging me to stay with them. So I did—only by a miracle—until hearing the one mile time. "5:55; 5:56."

I had nothing left. I began to walk, ready to drop out of the race.

A stranger then slowed his pace and yelled to me, "Come on! You can do it!" Those encouraging words helped me finish the race.

Our schedules resemble that 10k race. The frantic pace is symbolic of our lifestyle. We make no time to slow down. We fill our calendars with endless commitments and then frantically run from one engagement to another. We can't keep up with the pace. Our schedules are so tight five minutes of interruption can defeat us. It inevitably puts us five minutes behind for the rest of the day. With family, job, and extracurricular activities, we take on too much.

The same is happening with our youth in school. I know parents who were baffled by their high school sophomore's unusual behavior. Every evening she came home from volleyball practice, flopped down on her bed, and cried. She was involved in more extracurricular activities than she could possibly keep up with. I shared the parents' concern at the school board meeting and asked them to enforce their policy of no activities on Wednesday evenings or Sundays.

Teachers say the schedule provides less time for review than in the past. It results in more pressure to apply the curriculum immediately. Students find no time to digest the material. William Glasser recommends fifteen minutes during the school day for the child to use as free time.[1] He says, "I believe, therefore, that we should program our children and ourselves less completely than we do. We should allow for time off, some leeway, some slack in the day; never make it too tight."[2]

The perfectionist gets caught up in doing. The answer for any problem is simply to work harder. Marian Woodman says, "For the perfectionist who has trained herself *to do*, simply *being* sounds like a euphemism for nothingness, or ceasing to exist."[3] We learn the simple lesson that it's all right simply to be, without pushing ourselves to do.

Holidays are especially difficult for perfectionists. On those holidays we are expected to slow down and relax with family or friends. Well, I can't stand the absence of a goal to drive me, even on holidays! I have just enjoyed one of the best Christmases ever with my family, but I had to apply myself to slowing down to enjoy it. Like any perfectionist, it's not natural to change pace; we find it hard to slow down and relax.

The contrast between doing and being is best illustrated by Mary and Martha's encounter with Jesus (Luke 10:38–42). Mary sat at the Lord's feet and listened to Jesus. Martha, meanwhile, was "distracted by many tasks." Immediately she took her case to Jesus.

"Don't you care that my sister has left me to do all the work around here? Tell her to get busy."

Jesus answered, "Martha, Martha, you are worried and distracted by many things; there is need for only one thing. Mary has chosen the better part, which will not be taken from her."

This passage has been employed over the years to make a distinction between the active life of Martha and the contemplative life of Mary. Walter Hilton uses this scripture to assert that the contemplative life is on a higher plane spiritually.[4] Others including Teresa of Avila have seen the importance of both; "to give our Lord a perfect hospitality, Mary and Martha must combine."[5] Gregory of Nyssa suggested the following route to perfection: "Everyone that is perfect is first joined to an active life in productiveness, and afterwards united to a contemplative life in rest."[6]

Some monastic orders have interpreted this as an ongoing commitment to service for the active life or a life-time commission to monasticism for the contemplative. No matter how we interpret this passage, we could all benefit from sitting at the feet of Jesus, from listening to Him speak, from choosing the better way.

The Bible clearly presents a way out of our dilemma from this driven lifestyle. The creation account points out that God rested on the seventh day, blessed it, and *hallowed* it (Genesis 2:3). God's purpose was to set aside the Sabbath as a holy day as well as a day of rest. Another clue to its significance is found in Deuteronomy 5:14, "But the seventh day is a Sabbath to the Lord your God; you shall not do any work." John Oswalt proclaims that the Sabbath is a day to celebrate our relationship with God.[7] Karl Barth believes that God's intent is the same: that God ceases work "in order to be free for the fellowship with man, the object of His love, for the rejoicing and celebration of His completed work together with his son on earth, His festive partner."[8]

The Old Testament also refers to the sabbatical year, every seventh, when the fields were left untilled, and debts were cancelled (Leviticus 26:34). We are reminded of the importance of observing the Sabbath in Hebrews 4:9–11: "So then, a Sabbath rest still remains for the people of God; for those who enter God's rest also cease from their labors as God did from His. Let us make every effort to enter that rest...."

The Sabbath is intended to minister to the whole person. It is one day built into each week for re-creation. When observed as God intended, the Sabbath is also a built-in guarantee to control a hectic lifestyle. It is a day to proclaim the Sovereignty of God, a day to celebrate our relationship with God. Since perfectionism often leads to workaholic tendencies, if we are to proclaim the Sovereignty of God, if we are to admit we are creatures and point to God as Creator, we will observe the Sabbath. We need the Sabbath as a day to renew our relationship with God.

I just read about Christine, who found a positive change when she committed to observing the Sabbath. She found that God seemed to stretch her hours during the other six days of the week. Rather than returning to work on Mondays exhausted, she came back refreshed. She now uses Sundays to enjoy her children. What is her conclusion? "God had a reason for setting aside one day of rest out of seven: we need it to function effectively the other six."

Similar to the Sabbath is the concept of leisure. Derived from the Greek word, *skola*—from which we get the English word, *school*—it actually means "the freedom to learn." In its original definition, leisure means that we have an opportunity to contemplate. To discover the world around us. To use our imagination and our creativity. To stand back and reflect. To take time to celebrate. To allow the Spirit to be free to speak to us. In ancient times of Greek influence, it was a great privilege to be able to take time for these ventures. This was considered the beginning of wisdom; leisure was a great privilege.

How different from our understanding of leisure today! To the Greeks, leisure was never idle time. Leisure was not doing whatever I want. Never a diversion to call our attention away from God. Not free time to waste, to fritter away. Never an opportunity to run from work, to avoid our duties. Leisure was not a time to sit, hypnotized by the TV set. Never a time to feel pushed by an assembly line or production numbers. Leisure was not a time to feel exhausted by constant rushing, but a time to be refueled. What a shame that today even our vacations become a time to see how many activities we can cram in!

Most of us can pray, "Lord, forgive us for our failure to admit our human need for rest." While John Wesley has been an example for us in many ways, he sounds as compulsive as those of our day when he declares, "Leisure and I have parted company. I have resolved to be busy until I die."[9] And he was, preaching three sermons a day and riding over 250,000 miles on horseback. This constant busyness, however, did not help his family life.

Indeed, we could benefit by heeding the Hebrew translation of Psalm 46:10, "Relax and know that I am God. Relax and experience that I am God." Might we hear Jesus' words to His disciples: "Come away to a deserted place all by yourselves and rest a while" (Mark 6:31).

I remember listening to Larry Burkett on the radio, warning us against working too many hours a day. He told of his former workaholic lifestyle when he worked sixteen-hour days. Burkett stressed that he discerned he was able to accomplish more in an eight-hour day than he could previously in sixteen hours. He emphasized placing God and family above work and money in our priorities. He quoted the following verse as helpful: "It is in vain that you rise up early and go late to rest, eating the bread of anxious toil, for God provides for His beloved during sleep" (Psalm 127:2).

During the early 1900's, when manual labor was usually part of any employment, the Sabbath was observed. Laws allowing Sunday sports were not ushered in until the 1930's. Blue laws prohibiting

Sunday sales in any business were in effect in every village and city. Yet in our day consumerism and production have replaced former concepts of Sabbath and leisure.

We ask: How many products can I use at once? How can I do more tasks at one time? But multi-tasking won't close the gap between us and God.

Even our relationships are affected by this consumption mode. It becomes too easy to utilize people for what they can do for me, rather than actually working on building relationships. Instructions in Deuteronomy 15:7—11 ask us to give liberally to a needy neighbor, to open our hand to provide necessities for the poor. The implication is that God values people, not because of what they can do for God or because of social status, but quite simply because they are a major priority to God. God places no conditions on valuing each of us. Hopefully, we can follow God's example and value persons not because of social status but simply because they are of utmost importance to God.

To allow God to speak to us through the Sabbath and leisure demands that we overcome our complex of "instant gratification." It requires us to slow down, to be patient, to wait upon the Lord. Andrew Murray says, "True faith recognizes the need of time, and rests in God."[10] We can be assured that "those who wait upon the LORD shall renew their strength" (Isaiah 40:31).

One morning I sat down to make a list of everything I needed to accomplish that day—a sure sign of a perfectionist. Twenty-seven items! With reckless abandon, I plowed away at them. Interruptions hampered progress on any paperwork. But I persisted. To a perfectionist, no delight matches scratching through an item on the "to-do" list.

That evening I went to see a friend at the hospital. He was asleep, breathing by respirator. Angrily, frustrated, I muttered, "That's how the whole day has gone. Another wasted trip!"

But then a picture over his bed caught my eye. It portrayed a breath-taking mountain scene, along with this prayer from Michelangelo: "Lord, grant that I may never accomplish more than I desire."

I certainly hadn't accomplished more than I wanted. But this prayer suddenly changed my perspective. For in that instant I was no longer disappointed in what I hadn't accomplished that day. No, I was grateful for all twenty-seven items to work at during the next day. God had shown me there would be a fresh start in working on the same list the next day without looking back.

Thomas Kelly points to the Divine Center as he writes, "…"We have hints that there is a way of life vastly richer and deeper than all this hurried existence, a life of unhurried serenity and peace and power. If only we could slip into that Center! If only we could find the Silence which is the source of sound!"[11]

John Greenleaf Whittier wrote a poem entitled, "The Brewing of Soma," in 1872. This poem is Whittier's reaction against the loud, emotion-laden revivals and camp meetings that were popular in his day. The poem goes so far as to liken the noise to pagan religious rites. The well-known hymn, "Dear Lord and Father of Mankind," is taken from the last lines of Whittier's poem. Whittier's Quaker background and subsequent need for silence are evident in the last three verses of the hymn. Allow them to minister to our need for rest.

> O Sabbath rest by Galilee,
> O calm of hills above,
> Where Jesus knelt to share with Thee
> The silence of eternity,
> Interpreted by love!
>
> Drop Thy still dews of quietness,
> Till all our strivings cease;
> Take from our souls the strain and stress,
> And let our ordered lives confess
> The beauty of Thy peace.
>
> Breathe through the heat of our desire
> Thy coolness and Thy balm;
> Let sense be dumb, let flesh retire;
> Speak through the earthquake, wind, and fire,
> O still, small voice of calm.

CHAPTER SIXTEEN

The Mirror of Service

"…Christian leadership is accomplished only through service. This service requires the willingness to enter into a situation, with all the human vulnerabilities a man has to share with his fellow man."

—Henri Nouwen

"But be doers of the word, and not merely hearers who deceive themselves. For if any are hearers of the word and not doers, they are like those who look at themselves in a mirror; for they look at themselves and, on going away, immediately forget what they were like" (James 1:22—24). James, brother of our Lord, here reveals a negative aspect of the mirror. These are the ones who hear the word, but fail to put it into practice.

These "hearers who deceive themselves" remind me of public figures whose misdeeds are exposed by the media. A cloud of mistrust hovers as news travels detailing their scandals.

O. J. Simpson received more notoriety for evading the police in his white Ford Bronco on Interstate 405 than he ever did in escaping tacklers on the football field. Ninety-five million viewers watched the pursuit of a wanted man. Then many watched the trial that lasted nine months. He was acquitted in that trial, followed by losing a civil suit to the Brown and Goldman families, and later sentenced to 33 years in Nevada for robbery, weapons, and kidnapping.

President Bill Clinton denied any wrongdoing with Monica Lewinsky. After learning the truth, the House of Representatives voted to impeach Clinton, but the Senate reversed that.

Bernie Madoff confessed to building an elaborate Ponzi scheme, scamming numerous investors of an estimated $64.8 billion. He was sentenced to 150 years in prison.

Public officials are constantly on trial for extortion of public funds. We don't have to look very far in our own neighborhoods to see people reflected in this negative mirror.

In contrast—though James doesn't mention it—a positive mirror also appears. These are the people who take seriously the command to "be doers of the word." These are the faithful, dependable folks who put their faith into practice. They are seldom in the headlines, but more plentiful than those publicized by the media. Realizing the need for action, Jean de Caussade vowed, "I must not, like the quietists, reduce all religion to any denial of any specific action...."[1] Indeed, the positive mirror reveals actions of service.

This mirror does not run counter to contemplation, but complements it. Augustine wanted contemplatives "to devote themselves also to the external works of the apostolate, and to become *men of action*, without for that reason giving up their delight in God and truth."[2] Thomas Merton maintains, "The life of contemplation must spill over into action; much of that action is dialogue with others, and in that dialogue there must be much listening."[3] The very life of Christ reveals a rhythm between retreat and service, between ministering to one's own soul and ministering to others, between taking in and giving out.

In the book, *A Severe Mercy*, Sheldon Van Auken writes a moving love story relating the innermost struggles of his beloved as she is struck by a terminal disease. He too struggles. They celebrate a rich dialogue with C. S. Lewis and fellow students, combined with the opportunity to discover intellectual and spiritual frontiers. One evening a friend, Mary Ann, sums it up this way: "This, you know, is a time of taking in—taking in friendship, conversation, gaiety, wisdom, knowledge, beauty, holiness and later, well, there'll be a time of giving out."[4]

Jesus set the example for our service when He took the towel and basin and washed the disciples' feet. Even with His great authority—the authority to feed thousands, to heal the sick, to exorcise demons, to restore life to the deceased—Jesus washed the disciples' feet to demonstrate the need for service in the most menial of tasks. He then shows His authority by saying to His followers, "So if I, your Lord and Teacher, have washed your feet, you also ought to wash one another's feet" (John 13:14).

Jesus constantly reminds the disciples of their status as servants, of being sent out on a mission. No less than five times in the gospels we find this truth: "A servant is not greater than his Lord; neither one that is sent greater than the one who sent him" (for example, John 13:16). Walter Hilton understood this would not be easy, for he wrote, "But it is true that, of all the crafts, the service of God is the most sovereign and the most subtle, the loftiest and the most difficult to practice perfectly..."[5]

Jesus points out the way to true service; the gospel of success is controlled by a self-righteous service. In his book, *Celebration of Discipline*, Richard Foster distinguishes between true service and self-righteous service, as he says, "Self-righteous service comes through human effort. True service comes from a relationship with the divine Other deep inside."[6] Foster contrasts self-righteous service with true service in eight more contrasting statements:

"Self-righteous service is impressed with the 'big deal.'......True service finds it almost impossible to distinguish the small from the large service.

"Self-righteous service requires external rewards...... True service rests contented in hiddenness.

"Self-righteous service is highly concerned about results...... True service is free of the need to calculate results.

"Self-righteous service picks and chooses whom to serve . . . True service is indiscriminate in its ministry.

"Self-righteous service is affected by moods and whims...... True service ministers simply and faithfully because there is a need.

"Self-righteous service is temporary... . . . True service is a lifestyle.

"Self-righteous service is insensitive... . . . True service can withhold the service as freely as perform it."

"Self-righteous service fractures community... . . . True service, on the other hand, builds community."[7]

The highest priority in our mirror of service is to seek God's will in how we serve. While perfectionists seek to master or perfect any task, our focus is redirected as we seek to do God's will. The *Paster Noster*—or the Lord's Prayer—offers meaning to Evelyn Underhill as she explains: "I go back to the one perfect summary of man's Godward life and call—the Lord's Prayer. Consider how dynamic and purposive is its character. Thy will be done—Thy kingdom come! There is energy, drive, purpose in those words; and intensity of desire for the coming of perfection into life."[8]

The mirror of service calls us "to do justice, to love kindness, to walk humbly with our God" (Micah 6:8c-d). The servants of God are expected to offer compassion to the hungry and the homeless, the imprisoned and the ill, the alien and the bereaved. To do so, we must walk with God in humility; we depend upon God filling us with His love so that we can offer that love to the needy.

Centuries ago, a not-so-famous sheep rancher named Amos lived in Tekoa, south of Jerusalem. Although happy to tend his sheep and plant sycamore trees, he was no country hick. He was up-to-date on the latest news, understood history, and traveled the major roads of commerce. As he observed goods exchanged in business, he witnessed a plunge in morality. Many cheated to gain a luxurious lifestyle, while the poor starved. Merchants gave sacrifices and tithes at the Temple to manipulate God, to buy God's favor. Corrupt judges accepted bribes. Amos prophesied about the coming doom of "the day of the Lord" for the offenders. That prophesy says, "But let justice roll down like waters, and righteousness like an ever-flowing stream" (Amos 5:24).

"To do justice" requires us to care for the poor. When Rachel was in first grade, she told Glenda that she wanted to invite everyone in her class to her birthday party. Invitations were sent to all, including Pam, a needy classmate who lived in the trailer court and spoke with a speech impediment toward which her classmates showed no mercy.

As soon as the invitations were sent out, the popular kids began to pressure Rachel. They said, "If Pam comes, then I don't." Rachel told them to choose for themselves whether to come or not, but the invitation to Pam stood. All the popular kids (and Pam) showed up at the party. I was proud of Rachel for befriending Pam and for sticking to the original plan. She stood up to the pressure and did justice.

The mirror of service calls us to offer mercy. Jesus said, "Blessed are the merciful, for they shall receive mercy" (Matthew 5:7). More than anything else, perfectionists have difficulty with carrying this out because we feel we are being asked to lower our standards. How can we give anyone else some slack when we don't allow ourselves any? But mercy is mandatory for followers of Christ. Mahatma Gandhi says, "Only the admission of defect in oneself makes it possible for one to become merciful to others."[9]

The mirror of service calls us to live as faithful stewards. Unfortunately, perfectionists often fall into a competitive trap of trying to keep up with others in worldly goods. In the perfectionist's mind, a luxury becomes a necessity. Because of competing with a neighbor, the perfectionist often feels it a priority to have the latest, most luxurious home or most expensive car.

Centuries ago, the challenge of Jesus to perfection planted the seed for the ascetic teachings of monasticism.[10] About 270 A. D. Anthony, founder of monasticism, was on his way to church in the little hamlet of Koma, Egypt. He was feeling very unworthy. The gospel reading in church was from Matthew 19:21 where Jesus said to the rich young ruler: "If you wish to be perfect, go, sell your possessions, and give the money to the poor, and you will have treasure in heaven; then come, follow me." This Scripture inspired the foundation for the monastic order.

Later, other monastics such as Francis of Assisi would follow suit. Joseph Milosh includes others: "Mystics of all sorts, including the Desert Fathers and the members of the various sects prevalent by the fourth century after Christ, sought to achieve perfection partially rejecting the goods and consequently the cares of the world..."[11]

Although many of us struggle with finances, we could certainly live with much less than we have. Richard Foster advises us to de-accumulate.[12] In other words, Foster recommends that we rid ourselves of our many possessions. David Stoop went through everything he owned with his wife and asked two questions: (1) Do we need it? and (2) How does it add meaning to our lives?"[13] In this same vein Gregory of Nyssa says, "The measure of sorrow you experience in letting go of a thing is the measure of love you had in holding on to it."[14]

When floods, tornadoes, or hurricanes hit, victims are seen on television totally devastated, saying, "We lost everything."

Yet other victims say, "We still have all that matters to us: our family and our faith." Walter Hilton's words are immensely appropriate for our materialistic age: "To love and possess more than you reasonably need is a great fault."[15]

It is important for parents to model stewardship. I made it a practice to have our daughters put my check to the church in the offering plate. I wanted them to see stewardship as a priority and to peek to see if I was giving a generous gift. Later, a great joy of parenting arrives when we observe our children learn to give.

Rachel went two hours away from Cimarron to basketball camp during the summer before seventh grade. We gave her seventy dollars as spending money for the week. When we arrived to pick her up on Friday, she had spent a total of seven dollars. On the way back home we stopped at the mall. She shopped and then handed me a present: a baseball figurine with a music box that plays "Take Me Out to the Ballgame." Rachel hadn't forgotten the Sunday before was Fathers' Day when she had no money. She also bought presents for Glenda and Andrea and saved nothing for herself. She claimed the joy of giving!

Along this line of teaching stewardship to our children, Marjorie Holmes writes a meaningful prayer in a Christmas devotional. She prays, "Dear Lord, we weren't perfect parents. You know how often we failed our children; how miserable we often were, worrying about gifts we couldn't buy them. But now my heart overflows with thanksgiving. To realize we did give them something money couldn't buy or any camera record—the sheer wonder and joy of giving."[16]

In our deep commitment to stewardship, perfectionists sometimes go overboard to save a penny. How many times have we made ourselves sick eating twice as much as needed at an all-you-can-eat buffet? We paid the price; now we're determined to eat our money's worth. It's really not worth chasing slivers of soap in the shower or eating the crumbs in the bottom of the cereal box to save a little. I've eaten questionable leftovers from the refrigerator. It wasn't worth a belly ache. Between learning those lessons and dealing with perfectionists, I've learned it's okay to let the little things go.

The mirror of service calls us to build up the body of Christ, to work for unity. Like the physical body, "we, who are many, are one body in Christ, and individually we are members one of another" (Romans 12:5). Melvin Dieter wrote *The Holiness Revival of the Nineteenth Century*. There he observed that Daniel Warner of the Church of God in Anderson, Indiana longed for the unity of all Christians "not bound together by rigid articles of faith, but perfectly united in love, under the primitive glory of the Sanctifier..."[17]

The road to unity can trap us with dangers and detours. One specific entrapment is Kenneth Haugk's perception that antagonists in the church have tried to exploit "the perfectionist's tendency to blame him- or herself."[18] Unity in the church is shattered by the antagonist's attacks. The perfectionist is reluctant to stand up to the antagonist because of being too conscientious.

Another trap is our tendency to isolate ourselves. Thomas Merton, in his book, *No Man Is An Island*, reminds us that perfection cannot occur without interaction with others.[19] Yet he also stresses the need for solitude and that "individuals must perfect themselves so that the community can be perfected."[20]

Thankfully, we are not alone in our task. Evelyn Underhill lifts up the One who can strengthen us: "Yet we see in this muddled world a constant struggle for Truth, Goodness, Perfection; and all those who give themselves to that struggle—the struggle for the redemption of the world from greed, cruelty, injustice, selfish desire, and their results—find themselves supported and reinforced by a spiritual power which enhances life, strengthens will, and purifies character."[21]

Glenda had gone to the hospital to work the day shift as a nurse on a Sunday morning, and I was getting ready to make the bed when the phone rang at 7:00. My former seminary professor, Don Joy, was at the Wichita airport, flying standby, and hoping for a plane that afternoon to return home. I picked him up at the airport and brought him to the parsonage.

I walked to the bedroom, intent on making the bed. Don followed, and I apologized. "I'm sorry. I was just getting ready to make the bed when you called."

He went to the other side of the bed and started doing his part to help make the bed.

Then he offered to teach a Sunday School class at the church where I was pastor. He told the class, "I probably know a hundred people in Wichita, but there was only one name I thought of when I realized I would be spending some time in Wichita." In his role as servant, Don gave a glowing endorsement of me as pastor. More than once, Don Joy set an example of service that day. I'll always remember him as one who was willing to serve.

The mirror of service calls us to be "doers of the Word," to be willing to wash one another's feet. Let us serve by doing justice. We can serve others by offering them mercy. May we serve by living as good stewards of the world God has created. And we can serve most effectively by allowing the Holy Spirit to unite us in the body of Christ. Albert Schweitzer points to service as the means to happiness. He writes, "I don't know what your destiny will be: but one thing I do know: The only ones among you who will be really happy are those who have sought and found how to serve."[22]

CHAPTER SEVENTEEN

The Reflection of Perfection

"Regard yourself as clay in the hands of the Great Artist, spending all His thought and time and love to make you perfect."

—Andrew Murray

J. T. Seamands was my tennis partner during seminary. At sixty-one years of age, he still played in tournaments with the students. When we played each other in a singles tournament, he said, "If I win two sets, I go on. If you win two sets, you go on. If we split sets, you go on because I can't play three sets."

His wife once told J. T. that he was going to die on the tennis court.

He replied, "I can't think of a better way to go!"

And he was still playing tennis into his nineties.

J. T. Seamands was also my professor. When I received my grade on one of his essay tests, I was shocked. "Only 85! I deserve better than that!"

Later, I went to see J. T. Seamands. I told him of my disappointment and asked where I had gone wrong.

Without a moment's hesitation, he reached for my test with one hand and for a red pen with the other hand. He did not bother to look inside at any answers but briskly marked through the "85" and replaced it with "98." To this day his action still stirs me and not just because of the grade. He showed so much wisdom and grace. He was admitting that he could be wrong, that he was human. He was also saying that my test answers still weren't perfect.

More importantly, he was saying that our relationship mattered more to him than any test score. Grace was more important than following the letter of the law. God is surely like that!

You're giving your all to become perfect? God has already taken care of that need. The author of the book of Hebrews writes,

"For by one sacrifice He (Jesus Christ) has made perfect forever those who are being made holy" (10:14). God offers grace! Believers are perfect and being made holy at the same time.

Perfection isn't anyone's favorite topic of conversation. Mention it any time, and the response will be a cold stare or a deaf ear. Either "It took a lot of nerve to bring that up."

Or "I'm going to pretend I didn't hear that."

It reminds us of painful failures. Perfectionists are especially sensitive about the subject. It's discouraging to be reminded of that elusive goal that constantly defeats the perfectionist, a goal beyond the reach of any human.

More guilt and shame is not what we need. Quite the opposite. We need the gentle conviction of the Holy Spirit, we need God's forgiveness, and we need affirmation. We need the reassurance that in God's eyes we are accepted and approved, that we are whole and complete. We need grace!

When Rachel was five, we watched her favorite video, "Annie," fifteen times. Poor little Annie is kicked around and mistreated by the alcoholic Miss Hannigan. She yearns to leave the orphanage, longing to see her real parents. A turning point occurs when Daddy Warbucks says to her, "I love you like you were my own daughter." He also says, "But Annie, you are special."

Most of us need to hear those words more often. Since they are difficult to believe, say them softly: "I am special." Now that they've been said once, it's okay to say them louder: "I am special." Try to become familiar with them because they help during times when we are tested.

So many of the people I've counseled feel a void in being affirmed as a child. So many are hurting because they have never heard some extremely important words: "You are special." Or "I love you." Or "I'm proud of you." Those words cannot be said too many times by a parent or loved one. These ten words are the parent's Top Ten!

But what if you didn't hear them as a child? God has many creative ways to affirm us, even if we lacked loving support from parents, or still don't receive it from loved ones. God sometimes provides a surrogate in the church to fill that void. A person in the community might reach out through Big Brothers or Big Sisters.

The psalmist implies that God is working to help all who have this deep-seated longing for affirmation from parents. He says, "If my mother and father forsake me, the Lord will take me up" (27:10). The Lord cannot provide a comforting touch like a loved one, but can send someone our way who will. God has a loving heart for all who have been abandoned. The Bible says, "Father of orphans and protector of widows is God in His holy habitation" (Psalm 68:5). God has a special love for these who feel abandoned and alone.

Dr. Eben Alexander is a neurosurgeon trained to think in a scientific way. He was always convinced that there was a rational reason to explain all the stories he heard about people who had "near-death" experiences. He didn't believe their talk about heaven.

But Eben Alexander battled *E. Coli* bacteria that were eating away his brain. He was in a coma for seven days. He went through his own "life-after-life" event with a view of heaven. He is now sure heaven is real, writing openly of his time there. He received a message in heaven that came in three parts:

"You are loved and cherished, dearly, forever."

"You have nothing to fear."

"There is nothing you can do wrong."[1]

These words are God's top nineteen words. How the perfectionist needs to hear those words that in heaven there is nothing we can do wrong! How we need to hear that we are loved forever!

Perfectionists still living on this earth, however, need grace. My brothers and I stayed at the home of Aunt Grace when we were little. Aunt Grace fixed pancakes for breakfast. At home I was perfectly happy eating my pancakes with only butter on them.

When I told Aunt Grace that, she said, "How can you eat those dry old things without syrup?"

I tried one of Aunt Grace's pancakes. She was right. They needed syrup. The syrup was the grace for "those dry old things." I am thankful for Aunt Grace – who often was a model of grace – but even more thankful for God's grace. Everyone needs some grace. Especially perfectionists.

Three times, the apostle Paul prayed for his "thorn in the flesh" to be taken away. Many have speculated what that thorn may have been, but we really don't know for sure. Eventually, Paul hears God's answer: "My grace is sufficient for you" (II Corinthians 12:9). The pain might not be eliminated, but we need grace when it persists.

At the very time we feel some assurance, exactly when we are making some progress with this perfectionism, we discover more demands, more expectations. Squarely confronting us is this commandment of Jesus Christ: "Be perfect, therefore, as your heavenly Father is perfect" (Matthew 5:48). Surely Jesus would not thrust such a heavy perfectionism on us. Fortunately, this heavy demand shrinks into a much lighter load when we understand the context and intention in the original Greek language.

In the midst of the Sermon on the Mount, there is a pattern of Jesus repeating an Old Testament law and then telling the hearers how He fulfills that law. Jesus said, "You have heard that it was said, 'You shall love your neighbor and hate your enemy.' But I say to you, 'Love your enemies and pray for those who persecute you'" (verses 43–44). The reason given is "so that you may be the children of your Father in heaven" (45a).

The passage continues, "For if you love those who love you, what reward do you have? Do not even the tax collectors do the same? And if you greet only your brothers and sisters, what more are you doing than others? Do not even the Gentiles do the same?" (verses 46–47).

The context is clearly that of love. It is only through perfect love that we could love our enemies. To be children of the heavenly Father, we are asked to be perfect in our love.

The Bible implies we can never reach perfect conduct or perfect knowledge in this earthly life, but we can give perfect love. If you are given a choice of perfect knowledge or perfect love, which do you take? Consider those weary travelers on the yellow brick road in the movie, "The Wizard of Oz." The scarecrow looking for a brain is much better off than the lion searching for a heart. Would you rather deal with someone with a brain and no heart or someone with a heart and no brain? I'd rather relate to someone who has a heart. This passage commands us to have a heart, to be perfect in our love.

The word, "perfect,"—as it is used in Matthew 5:48—also means "complete in the sense of having accomplished the purpose for which we were created." It's really about arriving at maturity, about fulfilling our purpose. The Greek verb is also used in the future tense, implying that we will be perfect in the next life. Reiner Schippers clarifies in *The New International Dictionary of New Testament Theology*, "Christian life in the New Testament is not projected idealistically as a struggle for perfection, but eschatologically as the wholeness which a person is given and promised."[2] The word, eschatological, refers to end times. Schippers interprets that to mean we will be made perfect when end times arrive.

Come with me down a narrow Kentucky road to an immaculate, white house. The sign out front reads, "POTTERY." Inside, we watch the potter work. He reaches into his plastic bag, pulls out a lump of clay and places it on the potter's wheel. He adds some water and pounds the clay on the wheel.

While the wheel turns faster, sensitive hands shape and twist, push and pull the clay. The vessel looks perfect, but the potter stops and takes a small bit of clay from the wet pot. He throws it in a pile with other discarded clay. The potter has found an imperfection that, when fired in the kiln, would have ruined the pot. The potter starts over and makes sure the clay is perfect before it is fired.

Like clay in the potter's hand, God once wanted to reshape the people of Israel. In Jeremiah 18:4–6 we read, "The vessel he was making of clay spoiled in the potter's hand, and he reworked it into another vessel, as seemed good to him.

"Then the word of the Lord came to me: 'Can I not do with you, O house of Israel, just as the potter has done?' says the Lord. 'Just like clay in the potter's hand, so are you in my hand, O house of Israel.'"

Like the potter at the wheel, God reshapes our lives. We do have imperfections. But we are assured that God works at creating within us a perfect vessel. Our part is to offer the Potter control in shaping us as vessels.

John Wesley preached about the importance of making progress toward perfection. Yet he did not believe that we would ever arrive at sinless perfection in this life.[3] Wesley exhorted Christ's followers to press toward the mark of perfection, to persist in reaching for the goal. Wesley proclaimed the doctrine of holiness, but also said we never lose the need for Christ's forgiveness. Still today, pastors being ordained in the Wesleyan tradition are asked Wesley's question: "Are you going on to perfection?" We can give thanks that believers in Christ are "going on to perfection"!

After reading numerous authors on the subject of Christian perfection, this question always forms in the back of my mind: What is the practical application of all this? Although there are many different understandings of Christian perfection, the one point they all agree on is that the initiative for Christian perfection originates in God's hands. The process of perfection is initiated by a Perfect God—not by mere mortals.

What can we do about it? Andrew Murray answers that we can yield to the Holy Spirit; "Perfection, as the highest aim of what God in His great power would do for us, is something so Divine, Spiritual, and Heavenly, that it is only the soul that yields itself very tenderly to the leading of the Holy Spirit that can hope to know its blessedness."[4]

Created in God's image (Genesis 1:27), we are called to be a reflection of the character of God. "*Vir est imago Dei.*" According to Hilton, "That is, man is the image of God. He is made to the image and likeness of God... . . . inwardly in the powers of his soul."[5] La Rondelle grasps this *imago Dei* to be a love relationship between the Creator and the created, a "living communion and fellowship with God."[6]

Similarly, the New Testament calls for *imitation Christi*, an increasing reflection of the character of Christ, an imitation of Christ.

It is rooted in our identification with Christ's death and resurrection through baptism. Andrew Murray asserts, "We learn to take Him as our example."[7] Likewise, Murray says, "Both in his external life and in his inner disposition the perfected disciple knows nothing higher than to be as His Master."[8] Created in the image of God, we are called to imitate Christ.

After Christ returns to earth to receive his followers, the *telios*, or "final perfection" will occur. It alludes to a mirror described in I Corinthians 13:12: "But now we see in a mirror dimly, but then face-to- face." This mirror is also known as the *visio Dei*, the face-to-face vision of God.

That same passage continues, "Now I know only in part; then I will know fully, even as I have been fully known." The cloudy veil of divine knowledge will be uncovered. Only then can we reflect the face-to-face glory of Jesus Christ. We shall know and understand fully. Murray says, "Union with Christ in heaven will mean likeness to Christ on earth in that lamblike meekness and humility in which He suffered, in that Son-like obedience through which He entered the glory."[9] As perfection was God's original intention for us—lost by the fall—so is it God's final aim for us.

When Andrea and I play ball, I let her make the rules. We play inside in our unfinished basement, using a tiny leather-covered ball with beans inside. Andrea makes a bat by putting her hands together in an interlocking fist. We don't run the bases.

When she hits the ball right to me, I catch it for an out. But when I'm up to bat, the real game is to appear to try to hit the ball, but miss.

She is a picture of coordination, winning 12-4. You see, she will want to play again soon. Her motivation will be high to beat Dad again. But she won't win every time. Not because I have to win, but because life is learning to handle defeat, too.

Sometimes I wonder if God isn't like that. Doing well motivates us to try again. But if we won every game, it wouldn't be any fun. Part of life is learning to deal with defeat. And if anyone was perfect, would that person feel a need for God?

Until the coming of "final perfection," let us be mirrors that reflect the glory of Christ toward others. Let us look unto Christ, Who is called the "Perfecter of our faith" (Hebrews 12:2). May God help us to become a reflection of the only perfection: God represented in the flesh by Jesus Christ. Perfectionists don't need to work any harder, to struggle any longer. All we need to do is trust the grace of God. He stretches out His hand to offer His grace. Look in the mirror and see that the best reflection is the example of Christ.

As we allow God to move us closer to becoming a reflection of Christ, consider an illustration from a little book called *The Greatest Thing in the World*, by Henry Drummond. This little book is a commentary on the love chapter, 1 Corinthians 13. Drummond uses the illustration of shining light through a prism.[10] When the light appears on the other side of the prism, it is broken down into the colors of the rainbow: red, blue, yellow, orange, green, violet. Drummond says what comes into view on the other side of love are its attributes: patience, kindness, generosity, humility, courtesy, unselfishness, good temper, guilelessness, and sincerity.

Applying his picture a step further, compare the prism to Jesus Christ. The components of love are seen in us only when filtered through the love of Jesus Christ. This is the mirror we've been searching for, the mirror that reflects God's grace working in us.

C. S. Lewis sums up the Biblical understanding of perfection in grand fashion. He says, "On the one hand, God's demand for perfection need not discourage you in the least in your present attempts to be good, or even in your present failures. Each time you fall He will pick you up again. And He knows perfectly well that your own efforts are never going to bring you anywhere near perfection. On the other hand, you must realize from the outset that the goal toward which He is beginning to guide you is absolute perfection; and no power in the universe, except you yourself, can prevent Him from taking you to that goal."[11]

Did Andrea make any progress in conquering her perfectionism? While in another room in the basement, I overhear her playing with her Barbie dolls; she is oblivious to any world outside this play world. She sings, pretending the song is really Barbie's melody.

The words to her song go, "Sometimes I fail."

Over and over again: "Sometimes I fail."

The tune is not sad, but triumphant. A bouncy, happy song. Her lyrics, as well as the tune, say Andrea has dealt with her failures. Those failures aren't depressing, but joyous. She knows grace, the only mirror able to make the perfectionist happy.

NOTES

Chapter 1: "Hooked by Perfection"

[1] Every time a first name appears alone – no last name – in the book, it has been changed to protect confidentiality (except when referring to author's immediate family).
[2] David Burns, "The Perfectionist's Script for Self-Defeat," *Psychology Today* (November, 1980), p. 44.
[3] David Stoop, *Living with a Perfectionist* (Nashville, Tennessee: Oliver-Nelson Books, 1987), p. 16.
[4] *Ibid.*, p. 17.
[5] James Jolliff, *Too Much of a Good Thing or the Perils of Perfectionism* (Waco, Texas: Self Control Systems, 1980), p. 19.
[6] *Ibid.*, p. 17.

Chapter 2: "The Parental Push"

[1] Ellen Stern, *The Indispensable Woman: Beating the Perfection Addiction* (New York: Bantam Books, 1988), p. 78.

Chapter 3: "Lower the Bar (To a Height You Can Clear)"

[1] David Burns, *The New Mood Therapy* (New York: William Morrow and Company, 1980), p. 300.
[2] *Ibid.*, p. 303.
[3] Dan Gutman, *Baseball's Biggest Bloopers: The Games That Got Away* (New York: Penguin Books, 1993), p. 44.

4 Burns, *Feeling Good: The New Mood Therapy,* p. 323.
5 Carl Jung, *Analytical Psychology: Its Theory and Practice* (New York: Pantheon Books, 1968), p. 149.

Chapter 4: "Breaking up with Parental Control"

1 Miriam Adderholdt-Elliot, *Perfectionism: What's Bad about Being Good?* (Minneapolis, Minnesota: Free Spirit Press, 1987), p. 27.
2 Kevin Leman, as quoted in Adderholdt-Elliot, p. 7.
3 Stoop, p. 72.
4 *Ibid.*
5 *Ibid.,* p. 115.
6 *Ibid.,* p.75.
7 *Ibid.*
8 Karen Horney, *Neurosis and Human Growth* (New York: Norton, 1950), p. 18.
9 *Ibid.*
10 Marion Woodman, *Addiction to Perfection: The Still Unravished Bride* (Toronto: Inner City Books, 1982), p. 27.
11 *Ibid.,* p. 7.
12 Carol Van Klompenburg, *What To Do When You Can't Do It All* (Minneapolis, Minnesota: Augsburg, 1989), p. 121.
13 Jolliff, p. 44.

Chapter 5: "In Quest of a Mirror"

1 Horney, p. 18.
2 Horney, as quoted in Stoop, p. 63.
3 Althea Horner, *Object Relations and the Developing Ego in Theory* (New York: Jason Aronson, 1984), p.102.
4 Stoop, p. 65.
5 Gail Deutsch and Meghan Moore, ABC News, August 15, 2012.
6 *Ibid.*
7 *Ibid.*
8 *Ibid.*
9 *Ibid.*

[10] *Ibid.*
[11] *Ibid.*
[12] *Ibid.*
[13] *Ibid.*

Chapter 6: "The Mirror of Appearance"

[1] Richard Schwartz, Mary Jo Barrett, and George Saba, "Family Therapy for Bulimia," *Handbook of Psychotherapy for Anorexia and Bulimia*, ed., David Garner and Paul Garfinkle (New York: Guilford, 1985), p. 283.
[2] Minirth-Maier Clinic Radio Broadcast, November 23, 1993.
[3] National College Health Assessment, Spring, 2011.
[4] National College Health Assessment, Spring, 2011.
[5] *Ibid.*.
[6] *Ibid.*
[7] *Ibid.*
[8] Cherry Boone O'Neill, *Dear Cherry* (New York: Continuum, 1985), pp. 13–-15.
[9] Hilde Bruch, "Four Decades of Eating Disorders," *Handbook of Psychotherapy for Anorexia Nervosa and Bulimia*, ed. David Garner and Paul Garfinkel (New York: The Guilford Press, 1985), p. 15.
[10] Woodman, p.63.
[11] Susie Orback, "Feminist Psychoanalytic Treatment," *Handbook of Psychotherapy for Anorexia Nervosa and Bulimia*, ed. David Garner and Paul Garfinkel (New York: The Guilford Press, 1985), p. 105.
[12] *Ibid.*.
[13] *Ibid.*.
[14] Donald Joy, *Bonding: Relationships in the Image of God* (Waco, Texas: Word Books, 1985), p. p.111.
[15] Familysafemedia.com.
[16] Ibid.
[17] Ibid.
[18] Michael C. Quadland, "Private Self-consciousness, Attribution of Responsibility, and Perfectionistic Thinking in Secondary Erectile

Dysfunction," *Journal of Sex and Marital Therapy* 6, no. 1 (1980), 47–55.

[19] Leah Zerbe, "Being Imperfect Could Save Your Life," Rodale.com, September 28, 2010.

[20] Stoop, p. 105.

[21] Stoop, p. 103.

[22] William Johnson, "Sports and Suds," *Sports Illustrated* 69 (August 8, 1988), no. 6, p. 78.

[23] *Ibid.*, p. 78.

[24] *Ibid.*.

[25] Woodman, p. 29.

Chapter 7: "The Mirror of Performance"

[1] Miriam Adderholdt-Elliot, p. 27.

[2] www.campuscalm.com.

[3] *Ibid.*.

[4] *Ibid.*

[5] *Ibid.*

[6] *Ibid.*

[7] Stoop, p. 41.

Chapter 8: "Friendly Failures"

[1] Wikipedia.com.

[2] *Ibid.*.

[3] John Wooden, *They Call Me Coach* (Waco, Texas: Word Publishing Company, 1972), p. 178.

[4] Aaron Beck, as quoted by Stoop, p. 34f.

[5] Invention. Smithsonian.org/centerpieces/Edison/000_story.

[6] *Ibid.*

[7] www.johndcook.com/blog/2009/11/23/thomas-edisons-fire.

[8] Grantland Rice, *The Tumult and the Shouting* (New York: A. S. Barnes and Company, 1954), p. 60.

[9] *Ibid.*

[10] About.com Golf: Part of *The New York Times Company*.

[11] www.thinkexist.com/quotes/failures.

[12] ABC News, June 3, 2012.

[13] www.thinkexist.com/quotes/failure.

[14] *1994 Abingdon Preacher's Annual*, ed. John Bergland, "Here Am I," a sermon by Ronald Love, pp. 169—-170.

Chapter 9: "Last- Minute Dangers"

[1] Henry Wheeler Shaw, *www.stopprocrastinating.com*, quote no. 165.

[2] Olin Miller, *www.stopprocrastinating.com*, quote no. 18.

[3] Mark Twain, *www.stopprocrastinating.com*, quote no. 124.

[4] www.stevepavlina.com/articles/overcoming-procrastination.htm.

[5] James Michener, *www.stopprocrastinating.com*, quote no. 153.

[6] Elizabeth Kubler-Ross, *www.stopprocrastinating.com*. Quote no. 141.

[7] Chuck Swindoll, *www.stopprocrastinating.com*, Quote no. 169.

Chapter 10: "Side Effects"

[1] Kenneth Rice, "Perfectionists More Vulnerable to Depression" *Journal of American Psychological Association*, May, 2006, volume 37, number 5, page 14.

[2] *Ibid.*

[3] Gloria Rakita Leon, Philip C. Kendall, and Judy Garber, "Depression in Children: Parent, Teacher, and Child Perspectives," *Psychology* 8, Number 2 (1980), p. 221.

[4] Stephen Ilardi, *The Depression Cure: The Six-Step Program to Beat Depression without Drugs* (Cambridge, Massachusetts: Da Capo Lifelong Books, 2009), p. 4.

[5] *Ibid.*, p. 65f.

[6] Thomas Kelly, *A Testament of Devotion* (New York: Harper and Brothers, 1941), p. 123.

[7] Stoop, p. 106—-108. See also Jolliff, p. 83.

[8] *Ibid.*, p. 53.

9 Leah Zerbe, "Being Imperfect Could Save Your Life," Rodale.com, September 28, 2010.
10 *Ibid.*

Chapter 11: "Forgive Yourself!"

1 G. K. Chesterton, as quoted by Charles Allen, *Perfect Peace* (Old Tappan, New Jersey: Fleming H. Revell, 1979), p. 44.
2 P. T. Forsyth, *Christian Perfection* (London: Hodder and Stoughton, 1899), p. 1.
3 Walter Hilton, *The Stairway of Perfection*, M. L. Del Mastro, trans. (Garden City, New York: Image Books, 1979) p. 243.
4 Robyn Halley in news interview, Channel 6, KSBD, Ensign/Dodge City, Kansas, January 18, 1994.
5 *The Wichita Eagle* (Kansas), September 10, 1993, Page 5A.
6 *Ibid.*
7 Nicholas K. Geranios, Associated Press, August 20, 2012.
8 *Ibid.*
9 *Ibid.*
10 Philip Yancey, *Reaching for the Invisible God* (Grand Rapids, Michigan: Zondervan, 2000), p. 193.
11 M. Scott Peck, *People of the Lie* (New York: Simon and Schuster, 1983), p. 71.

Chapter 12: "Forging Friendships"

1 Woodman, p. 188.
2 Paul Rom, "The Misery of Perfectionism," *Individual Psychologist* 8 (May, 1971), p. 8.
3 *Ibid.*
4 Stoop, p. 15.
5 Adderholdt-Elliot, p. 41.
6 Stoop, p. 95.
7 Jolliff, p. 18.
8 Harriet Lerner, *The Dance of Intimacy* (New York: Harper and Row, 1989), p. 215.

9 Augustus Napier and Carl Whitaker, *The Family Crucible* (New York: Harper and Row, 1978), p. 93.

10 Henri Nouwen, *The Wounded Healer* (New York: Doubleday, 1978), p. 71.

11 *Ibid.*, p. 71f.

12 E. M. Pattison, *Pastor and Parish*, as quoted in Joy, p. 3.

13 Hans K. La Rondelle, *Perfection and Perfectionism: A Dogmatic-Ethical Study of Biblical Perfection and Phenomenal Perfectionism*, (Barrien Springs, Michigan: Andrews University Press, 1971), p. 117.

Chapter 13: "Embracing God"

1 Jolliff, p. 81.

2 Will Rogers, as quoted in Stoop, p. 60.

3 Nouwen, p. 93.

4 La Rondelle, p. 26.

5 Thomas à Kempis, *Of the Imitation of Christ* (Grand Rapids, Michigan: Baker, 1973), p. 27.

6 Thomas Wilson, as quoted in Frederick Kates, *Moments with the Devotional Masters* (Nashville: The Upper Room, 1961), p. 54.

7 George Fox, as quoted in Kates, p. 50.

8 Andrew Murray, *Be Perfect! A Message from the Father in Heaven to His Children on Earth* (New York: Anson D. F. Randolph and Company, 1893), p. 8.

9 Evelyn Underhill, *The Spiritual Life* (New York: Harper and Row, 1936), p. 55.

10 John Wesley, *A Plain Account of Christian Perfection* (Kansas City, Missouri: Beacon Hill Press, 1966), p. 113.

11 Jean-Pierre de Caussade, *The Sacrament of the Present Moment*, Kitty Muggeridge, trans. (San Francisco: Harper and Row, 1982), p. 31.

12 *Ibid.*, p. 42.

13 Murray, p. 26.

14 P. T. Forsyth, *Christian Perfection* (London: Hodder and Stoughton, 1899), p.1.

[15] La Rondelle, p. 38.

[16] Murray, p. 111.

[17] De Caussade, p. 53.

[18] Mary Mason, *Active Life and Contemplative Life: A Study of the Concepts from Plato to the Present* (Milwaukee, Wisconsin: The Marquette University Press, 1961), p. 58.

[19] Laurence Wood, *Pentecostal Grace* (Wilmore, Kentucky: Francis Asbury Publishing Company, 1980), p. 184.
The doctrine of dispensations holds that God has divided history into specific periods of time and that God reveals Himself to humanity through unique, specific ways in each biblical period.

[20] Ives Congar, as quoted by Wood, p. 27.

[21] Constance Garrett, ed. *The Cloud of Unknowing* (Nashville, Tennessee: The Upper Room, 1961), p. 19.

[22] C. S. Lewis, *The Joyful Christian* (New York: MacMillan Publishing Company, 1977), p. 77—78.

[23] Ibid., p. 77.

[24] Kelly, p. 114.

Chapter 14: "Enjoy This Moment"

[1] de Caussade, p. 43.

[2] *Ibid*, p. viii.

[3] *Ibid*, p. 52.

[4] Murray, p. 91.

[5] De Caussade, p. 21.

[6] Jolliff, p. 90.

[7] Frances Touchet, "Perfectionism in Religion and Psychotherapy: Discerning the Spirits," *Journal of Psychology and Theology* 4, no. 1 (Winter, 1976), p. 25—26.

[8] Charles L. Allen, *God's Psychiatry* (Old Tappan, New Jersey: Fleming H Revell Company, 1953), p. 14.

[9] William Ward, *The Divine Physician* (Richmond, Virginia: John Knox Press, 1966), Morning 12.

[10] William Law, *A Serious Call to Devout and Holy Life*. Aas quoted in Kates, p. 55.

11 Woodman, p. 66.

12 Adderholdt-Elliot, p. 58.

13 Jacob M. Braude, *Speakers and Toastmasters' Handbook of Anecdotes by and about Famous Personalities* (Englewood: New Jersey: Prentice-Hall, 1971), p. 113.

14 Norman Cousins, *Anatomy of an Illness*, as quoted in Allen Klein, *The Healing Power of Humor* (Los Angeles: Jeremy P. Tarcher, Inc., 1989), p. 18.

15 Elton Trueblood, *The Humor of Christ* (New York: Harper and Row, 1976), p. 15.

Chapter 15: "A Leisurely Pace"

1 William Glasser, *Positive Addiction* (New York: Harper and Row, 1976), p. 136.

2 Ibid., p. 137.

3 Woodman, p. 84.

4 Hilton, p. 124.

5 Saint Teresa, *Moradas Setinus*, as quoted in Evelyn Underhill, *Mysticism*, p. 514.

6 Gregory of Nyssa, *Moralia Epistola Missoria*, vi, 61, PL75, 764.

7 John Oswalt, "The Minister and Leisure," March 8, 1982, La Mesa, Texas. Much of what is stated here is dependent upon Oswalt's lectures.

8 Karl Barth, *Church Dogmatics*, ed. G. W. Bromiley and T. F. Torrance, III, 1, Edinburgh, p. 215.

9 John Wesley, as quoted by Oswalt.

10 Murray, p. 114.

11 Kelly, p. 115.

Chapter 16: "The Mirror of Service"

1 De Caussade, p. 46.

2 Cayre, *La Contemplation Augustine* (1927), pp. 331–332.

[3] Thomas Merton, as quoted in Robert Voigt, *Thomas Merton: A Different Drummer* (Liquori, Missouri: Liquori Publications, 1972), p. 99.

[4] Sheldon Van Auken, *A Severe Mercy* (New York: Bantam Books, 1977), p. 116.

[5] Hilton, p. 232.

[6] Richard Foster, *Celebration of Discipline* (New York: Harper and Row, 1978), p. 112.

[7] *Ibid*, pp. 112—113.

[8] Underhill, *The Spiritual Life*, p. 77.

[9] Mahatma Gandhi, quoted by Thomas Merton, *Gandhi on Nonviolence*, p. 12.

[10] William Greathouse, *From the Apostles to Wesley* (Kansas City, Missouri: Beacon Hill Press, 1979), p. 51.

[11] Joseph Milosh, *The Scale of Perfection and the English Mystical Tradition* (Madison, Wisconsin: The University of Wisconsin Press, 1966), p. 24.

[12] Foster, p. 80.

[13] Stoop, p. 143.

[14] Gregory of Nyssa, *Moralium Libri Sive Exposito in Librium b. Job*, I, 5, PL75, p. 531.

[15] Hilton, p. 161.

[16] Marjorie Holmes, *Daily Guideposts 1992* (Carmel, New York: Guideposts Associates, 1991), p. 343.

[17] Melvin Dieter, *The Holiness of the Nineteenth Century* (Metuchen, New Jersey: Scarecrow Press, 1980), p. 250.

[18] Kenneth Haugk, *Antagonists in the Church* (Minneapolis, Minnesota: Augsburg Press, 1988), p. 158.

[19] Thomas Merton, *No Man Is An Island*, as quoted in Voigt, p. 98.

[20] *Ibid.*, p. 94.

[21] Underhill, p. 110.

[22] Albert Schweitzer, www. famous-quotes.com/service.

Chapter 17: "The Reflection of Perfection"

[1] Eben Alexander, *Proof of Heaven: A Neurosurgeon's Journey into the Afterlife* (New York: Simon and Schuster Paperbacks, 2012), p. 71.
[2] Reiner Schippers, "Goal," *New International Dictionary of New Testament Theology*, Colin Brown, ed. *et al.*, II (Grand Rapids, Michigan: Zondervan, 1976), p. 65.
[3] A. Skevington Wood, *The Burning Heart, John Wesley: Evangelist* (Exeter, Devonshire, England: Paterrnoster Press, 1967), pp. 268–269. Wood, however, finds an instance where Wesley supports sinless perfection. "…A Christian is so far perfect, so as not to commit sin" (from Wesley's sermon entitled "Christian Perfection."). Found in *Sermons,* Vol. II, p. 169, Sermon XXXV. Wood says it depends on whether Wesley was emphasizing holiness or the need for progress toward perfection as to which way he decided.
[4] Murray, p. 8.
[5] Hilton, p. 191.
[6] La Rondelle, p. 68.
[7] Murray, p. 91.
[8] *Ibid.*, p. 53.
[9] *Ibid.*, p. 126.
[10] Henry Drummond, *The Greatest Thing in the World* (London: Collins, 1887), p. 26.
[11] Lewis, p. 78.

ABOUT THE AUTHOR

 Dan E. Ferguson has earned a doctorate in pastoral counseling from Graduate Theological Foundation and a bachelor's degree in religion and philosophy from Friends University in Wichita, Kansas. He worked as a chemical engineer, secondary school teacher, and sales representative before attending Asbury Theological Seminary, where he worked at ten different jobs before graduation. He has served as pastor to ten United Methodist Churches in Kansas. He currently lives in Wichita and serves the Douglass United Methodist Church. He has enjoyed starting contemporary worship services.

Dan is a sports fanatic; church attenders can count on a sports story in every sermon. He has logged enough miles to bicycle around the world twice (only one crash), run around the world once (only one dog bite), and walk around it twice (never hit by a golf ball). He has rooted for baseball teams in seventeen major-league stadiums. He has too many favorite sports teams and athletes to list them all. He feels blessed by love from thousands of parishioners and the opportunity to counsel hundreds. His congregation affirms that "he loves people of all ages." Dan appreciates support from his wife, Glenda; two daughters, Rachel and husband, Kevin Steiner; and Andrea and husband, Jeff Shultz; and a grandson, Bentley Steiner.

CPSIA information can be obtained
at www.ICGtesting.com
Printed in the USA
FFOW03n1104150118
44454874-44248FF

9 781640 828100